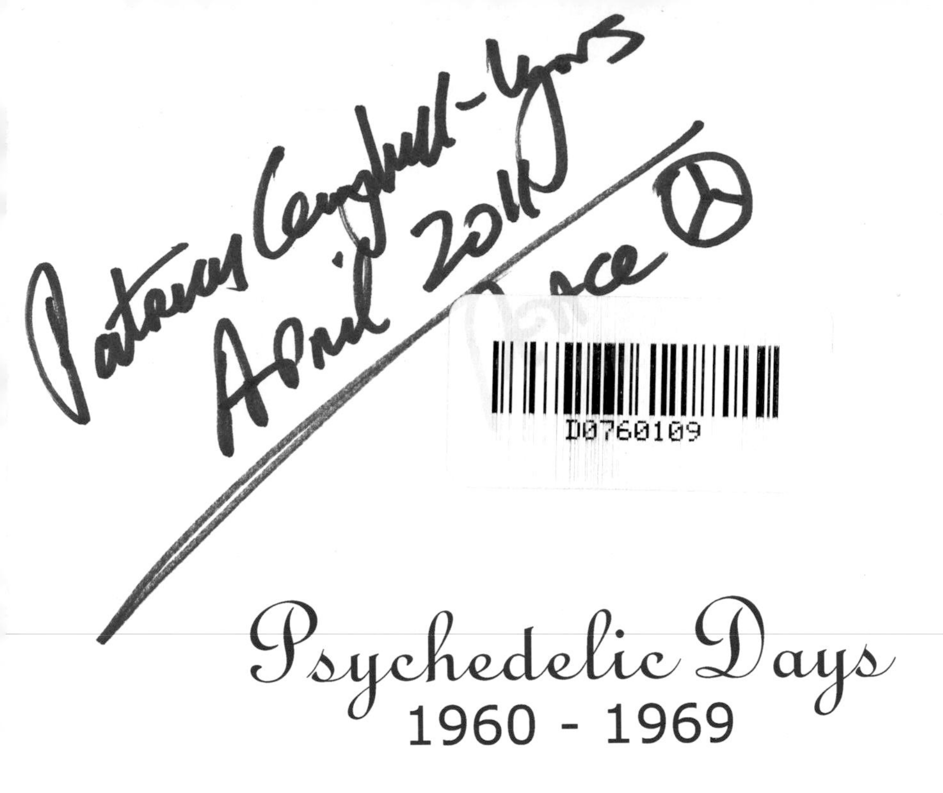

Psychedelic Days
1960 - 1969

by

Patrick Campbell-Lyons

This book is dedicated to those I love.

Psychedelic Days

AN INTRODUCTION
(Before and Beyond)

For me and Nirvana, the '60s were a trip indeed. Immigration blues, Paddies, navvies, booze, dope deals, thrills and pills, rhythm & blues, guitars and groupies, Mods and Rockers, free love and flower power, bohemian swagger boys and gypsy princesses, Ealing Art College, the local scenesters at Jim Marshall's Music Store in Hanwell, Speedy Keen, Mitch Mitchell, John McVie, Cliff Barton, Jimmy Royal, Ron Wood and Kim Gardner with the Birds, the boss guitar man Terry Slater, Pete Townshend, Pete Meaden, Vic Griffiths (the best harp player in West London), the legendary Ealing Club, the Rolling Stones, the Speakeasy in Margaret Street W1, the Limbo Club in Soho, the Bluebeat Jukebox, Blackbombers in Hyde Park, 51 Club Great Newport Street, La Gioconda Café, Denmark Street and the Tin Pan Alley publishing houses, Regent Sound,

St. Martins, the musical *Hair*, *You Can All Join In*, Jimi Hendrix, Guy Stevens, Mickie Most, Hamburg's Star Club, Paris, Belgium, Rio de Janeiro with Jimmy Cliff, Stockholm, Tangiers and the "happenings" of Morocco, Island Records and Chris Blackwell, Alex Spyropoulos and I creating the band Nirvana.

Oh yes, Nirvana—the first U.K. band to sign to Island in 1967, when the label released our now cult-status album *The Story of Simon Simopath*, one of the first concept albums ever recorded. Nirvana—the first group to use phasing on a complete track, our hit single "Rainbow Chaser"; the only British group to perform live with Salvador Dali; a group that, with arranger Syd Dale, made innovative use of orchestrated strings and brass in our recordings. In the studio, we worked with producers Jimmy Miller, Chris Blackwell, Tony Visconti, Muff Winwood, Chris Thomas and Brian Humphries, with bass player Herbie Flowers, with drummers Clem Cattini and Barry Morgan, with female vocalists Sue and Sunny, Madeline Bell, Kay Garner and Lesley Duncan. "I get high with a little help from my friends," Sue and Sunny sang on Joe Cocker's single, and I get high now 40 years later thinking about that global array of talent.

In 1969, an American man walked on the moon . . . We were there waiting for him.

* * *

I was born in small-town Ireland. "Townies" we were called provocatively by the boys from the countryside who cycled in to school every day. My parents were country people who left the land when they married and started our family, which would be supported and educated in the town, where my father secured a job, and where the Christian Brothers and the nuns taught school.

The town they chose to settle in was halfway between their respective homelands, a distance of 36 miles; it was also the place where they met every Sunday for the purpose of getting to know each other—"courting" it was called in those days of yore. The couple would cycle the 18 miles there and back to have a few precious hours in each other's company. When my father's proposal of marriage was accepted by my mother and her two brothers, he bought a car, an old Wolsley, then drove all the way to her home.

My own world was turning out to be quite a different place. After my education was completed, I said my goodbyes and sailed all the way into 1960s London.

On the boat to England, I thought about how my parents had sometimes struggled to offer my sister, my brother and me the best education available, giving us a strong sense of respectful independence, which we keep today. Our parents loved to go dancing and were members of the local amateur dramatic society. Music was always around; sometimes musical instruments were brought to our house. We were encouraged to write poems and sing songs, often in our own language.

I thought also about a friend in my class at school, the son of a local dance-band leader. He had a guitar, and had been to London once when his dad's orchestra was invited to play a gala ball at the Irish Center on St. Patrick's Day. I had a big crush on his gorgeous sister, but there was no chance there—she was going steady with someone else.

By the time the ferry boat arrived in Fishguard, from where I would take the train to Paddington, London, all my thoughts and longings had evaporated into the mist and fog of the swollen Irish sea. I had no fears for what lay ahead, but what I did have was a great sense of freedom. I was 18.

Everything changed for me in London as I discovered the bright lights of Ealing Broadway and the pubs on the Uxbridge Road of West Ealing and Hanwell. My '60s trip had begun.

* * *

In a 2009 issue of the highly rated British music publication *Mojo* celebrating 50 years of Island Records, I read, "on *The Story of Simon Simopath*, the album's second track "Lonely Boy" proved that Nirvana was ahead of its time in more than just its name . . ." I could not have said it better myself.

In early July of 2008, I started to write some songs and ideas about my life in '60s London and how I arrived there. A considerable passage of time had gone by, and I felt the words might be hard to find. But something happened that I can only describe as crystal karma vision. I was remembering with amazing detail those psychedelic days when I navigated my way on a voyage of music, freedom, adventure, self-discovery and loss. That part of my past had no distance; I was living it again. When I stopped writing four months later, I had a book.

Over the years and especially in this present decade, I have been asked on numerous occasions by people of all ages, "What were the '60s really like? Were they as beautiful and crazy as some people have written? Others say, "I wish I had been there." Well, my story is for all of you, but it is also for those who were there and did not make it to the other side.

Enjoy the trip!

Patrick Campbell-Lyons
May 2009

. . . AND I COULD HEAR THE MUSIC
My Upbringing, 1943-1960

Lady Luck had nothing whatsoever to do with my articulate conception. I was the product of shared longings—a late harvest, an impatient embryonic specimen confined in the annexe of existence while my Mam and Dad danced to the music of the Mick Delahunty orchestra. Mam was out of breath after a foxtrot that became a quickstep that turned into the conga. A few minutes later, Dad took her outside to the treasured Wolsley, where she put her feet up on the back seat and he wiped her face with his pressed white handkerchief. They smiled at the stars in a Tipperary sky—a proud man of coastal West Waterford, a strong woman from Cashel's agricultural heartland . . . and I could hear the music in the dance hall.

* * *

"He's kicking me," screamed my mother. I gave

her another couple of prods so that she would know for sure this was going to be a serious business. Overcome with a desire to get home, she urged Dad to put his foot down, but his laid-back, unflappable restraint kept the Wolsley at 30 mph. "I think he's coming, Tom," she roared, not knowing who she was mad at—the little fellow inside, or the big fellow outside, driving calmly and going steady. In the crowded parlour back home, the relations sat around, preparation holding hands with expectation, ignorance facing indoctrination, all of them tossing out the verbals like free tickets to the flicks on a Monday night. No one there gave a thought to the possibility that "he" might just be a "she." I could hear Jim Reeves singing . . . "Put your sweet lips a little closer to the phone."

* * *

As the afternoon waited for the evening to come, I crashed through the forest like a bullet from a gun. I shot through the sunlit frames on my new bike, screaming the bandleader's daughter's name, the same name as my mother's and the Blessed Virgin's . . . "Mary!" I screamed, and the echo reverberated off the leafy canopy into the lap of the day that had started with my serving mass on the Franciscan altar and would climax in the back row of the Ritz Cinema with passionate fumbling later in the evening. I could hear Connie Francis on the jukebox singing . . . "Lipstick on your collar, gonna tell on you."

* * *

I guaranteed my place in the small-town Hall of Fame when I threw a blow, in self-defence, at a Christian Brother, my Latin teacher, a bully and a fully paid-up member of the Cicero Club, a predator in the classroom and a sexual abuser in our homes. His name was Brother X, and his corrupt ways marked many of his pupils for years (though I forgave him many years ago). Unaware of the blackmail and repressed emotion that was involved, my mother said that I had committed a sacrilege. I knew the meaning of the word very well: "disrespect to a sacred person or thing," as we had it drummed into our ears every day. I had brought shame on our family. I had blotted my copybook in a serious way, and for a long time I stayed well clear of the clergy, always finding excuses or going on the missing list when volunteers were wanted for the playing fields or the church. It was a difficult time, as the men with the back-to-front collars had their eyes and ears everywhere in the town; their word was always sacred. I could hear Brenda Lee singing "Sweet Nothin'" on the radio.

* * *

Depending on my touch sensitivity and the weather in the Irish Sea, I was always looking forward to tuning in Radio Luxembourg on 208 medium-wave band every Sunday night for the "Top Twenty Show." As a family we always said the Rosary after dinner, the process always the same: turn our chairs around and kneel on the floor with our elbows resting where our arses had been, and each of us—my sister, brother, Mam, Dad and myself—said a decade each. It would take just under a half hour to complete, respecting the spiritual sentiment of every prayer, and I always made it up to my bedroom in time to turn on and tune in for my own Holy Hour. I could hear the Everly Brothers singing "Cathy's Clown." I looked at my reflection in a cracked mirror. I was wearing a suit of shimmer and light; my hair was on fire; a shower of sparks cascaded around me like a golden arch of neon on Broadway. I made shapes; I marched in the crossfire of the "Soldiers' Song"; I played in the "Garden of Temptation"; I lived like Tony Curtis; I talked like Jack Palance. I would not seek forgiveness from bigots, rogues and charlatans, or extend courtesy to chancers consumed by greed. It was time to go, time to leave behind the monuments of my short history and find a new adoration of the spirit. That night when I spoke to God, He knew that I was praying; when God answered me, I could hear Elvis singing "It's Now or Never."

Patrick Age 4

HAIR TODAY AND GONE TOMORROW

I started school when I was 4 years young, and my first day turned out to be one of confusion and curtailment. When my mam and I arrived at the convent gates, the nuns of the presentation order were waiting for us with open arms. All around us was pandemonium—screaming children being dragged redundantly down the street, others jumping out of their skins, galloping ahead eager to get into the austere building and be inducted on the blackboard of indoctrination.

In no time at all, the nuns took control of things. We were herded into the playground, sad mammys waving at us from outside the railings; the holy penguins were now in charge. I was wearing short grey trousers, a red-and-grey Fair Isle sweater my mam had knitted, starched white shirt with a crimson red tie, brown sandals, and grey knee-length socks—the same uniform as all the others. However, my distinguishable feature as a boy was my shoulder-length hair, a mass of curls awaiting the first appearance of the clippers. Perhaps the lack of shearing had to do with the fact that when relatives, neighbours and sometimes, when our family went into town, complete strangers, saw me for the first time, their instant observation was, "Look at the lovely head of curls, just like his daddy." My parents were not ready for the painful task of giving me a "short back and sides," the "pudding bowl" cut, as I often heard it described later in my youth.

We followed the nuns into the hall of the convent, where Reverend Mother Philomena stood up in front of us. "Now, boys and girls, we will say our prayers. Our father who art in heaven, hallowed be thy name . . ." the chorale of soaring voices ricocheted off the stone walls. Mother Philomena told us to remain standing and be perfectly quiet while Sisters Geraldine and Ursula would separate us, boys to the left, girls to the right, then you will go to your classrooms in the name of the Father, the Son and the Holy Ghost Amen, she made the sign of the cross on us in slow motion.

t was chaos as 40 of us, milling around trying to find left and right and everywhere in between, confused one another and Sisters Geraldine and Ursula, who were pushing and prodding us in the right directions. I was on the boys' side when I was grabbed by Sister Geraldine, who jet-propelled me to the other side. Before I could say boo to a goose, I was in the girls' classroom, too frightened to open my mouth as Reverend Mother had told us not to speak unless spoken to. Sister Geraldine began the story of Noah and the ark; when she came to the part where the animals went in two by two, she stopped and said, "Two by two—that is how I want you to go to your desks, and no talking or running." The first rule of the class was to raise your hand up high if you wanted to say something or attract her attention: "Hands up if you understand," and we obediently did what she expected.

I was becoming more nervous by the minute and

realised I was about to pee myself. I was in the second row; all the hands were up, everyone eager to give names to Sister Geraldine as she started to write them on the blackboard starting from the front row.

The floodgates opened above and down under. Sister Geraldine soon became aware of my predicament, rushed me outside to the bathroom and discovered to her astonishment that I was a boy and my name was Patrick. I was taken to Reverend Mother's office, and whispered words were exchanged with the high command. "Now, Patrick, we shall say no more about this unfortunate episode. Tomorrow you will start school again in the boys class." The Reverend Mother stroked my head as she spoke the reassuring words, "And we will contact your mother, so until she arrives you will come with me to the choir practise." A short while later, I was sitting to her left as she played the harmonium for the primary girls. My first job in music was to turn the pages of the hymn book towards me when she gave a slow downward movement of her head. Her saintly fingers played the celestial notes, while underneath, her feet pumped the pedals. It was magical, and for weeks my head was filled with the sanctified sounds of glorification.

That night my dad took out the angry clippers, and my mam stood close at hand holding the scissors. Later she cried as she collected the curls off the newspaper on the floor and put them away in a shopping bag at the back of the wardrobe, where they remained 10 years later. I went back to school the next morning, to the boys class; Sister Ursula was there to meet me and make sure all was in order.

On my desk I found a kaleidoscope, a present from God and the nuns with images of the Stations of the Cross inside. Sister Ursula told me, "The other boys had theirs yesterday, but I kept it for you, because it has your name on it, and I knew you were starting today." "I was here yesterday," I said, "but I was a girl." The class jeered and laughed until reprimanded by Sister Ursula.

Twenty years later, when my band the Second Thoughts shared the bill with the Pretty Things and the Downliners Sect on the London rhythm & blues circuit, my hair was down beyond my shoulders again. But when I saw from behind the extraordinary length of hair on Phil May and

Don Crane, the lead singers, I honestly thought they were girls.

ACROSS THE POND
My early days in London and the Second Thoughts, 1962-65

The Irish are an island people in every sense of the word. As a youngster I often heard the older ones say, "So and So went off across the water; it was a sorry day to see them go."

Which water did they mean? It was accepted in the famine days of 1845 to 1847 that the people from the western counties of Kerry, Clare, Galway, Mayo and Donegal went across the Atlantic Ocean waters to make a new and better life in the cities of Boston, New York, Chicago, Pittsburgh, Philadelphia and Baltimore, while the sons and daughters of Wicklow, Dublin, Wexford, Waterford and Cork were more likely to cross the pond to Liverpool, Birmingham, London, Leeds, Northampton and Manchester, where, according to an uncle of mine, the streets were not paved with gold, but if you worked hard and minded your own business, you would do well for yourself. This was the generation of my own father and his father before him, and now I was crossing the pond for the first time. I was 18 years, a man and about to discover my own personal gold.

I worked at Walls Ice Cream factory in Perivale, Middlesex, from July 1st to the end of September in the summer of 1961. I packed Vanilla Gold ice cream ten hours a day, six days a week, and you could get overtime. As a matriculated student waiting for a place in a college or university, I made what to me was a small fortune. The factory employed over 100 Irish students every summer, all hoping to save some money and make a serious contribution to the next year's college fees and living expenses; parents would have to make up the rest. The students would repeat the process over the following four years unless they got something better at home.

I rented a small bed-sitter in West Ealing—Melbourne Avenue, to be precise—with another student from my town. We paid six pounds a week rent; the gas and electricity were on a meter. I did not know it then, but this was to be the only time that I worked at something other than music, and the only experience I have ever had of receiving an envelope with my name and my work number printed inside the window, and a small wedge of notes and some coinage—my wages for a 60-hour week. (A couple of times I did the 72-hour week, with the overtime.) The idea of eating ice cream never crossed our minds; it meant nothing other than money.

I received my wages every Thursday. And every Thursday night, the only night of the week I went out, I would go to a pub called the Coach and Horses on the Uxbridge Road between West Ealing and Ealing Broadway, with a specific amount in my pocket for the purpose of getting lashed. Closing time would arrive with the ringing of the bell and "Time, gentlemen, please . . ." (What was that all about? If you did that in a pub in Ireland, you'd be out of business the next day.) I would weave my merry way up the

Uxbridge Road, or I might try to jump on a 207 to the Inishfree Dance Hall at the Broadway, where you would hear the most awful country showband dance music. I would attempt to dance with the first girl who said "yes" to my request, and for the rest of the night would try to convince her that she was the right girl for me and that she would be doing the right thing by letting me take her home, to my place or hers, either would do fine. I got warned off a few times by the management for what they called "messin'" and by the end of the night I could hardly stand up, never mind dance, or see clearly the face or the body of the girl I wanted to take home . . . But I did score on a couple of occasions.

On one Thursday night towards the end of September, a cocky young Irish fellow with a red electric Hofner guitar came onstage during the interval and played and sang three rock-and-rollers. I thought he was a thousand times better than the ten-piece showband. Later, I made myself known to him and stood him a drink. We became instant friends; I called him Clare—that was the county he came from. He called me Cork, even though I came from Waterford, the neighbouring county. It must have been my accent (I was born close to the Cork border), or it just sounded better for him, but I was stuck with it for a while.

Clare was a permanent fixture on the London landscape of construction sites, and I used to rib him: "You'll never go back now." He took me to hear two up-and-coming local bands, Frankie Reid and the Casuals and Jimmy Royal and the Hawks. I was instantly hooked by the music, the stage presentation and the bands' "girl followers"; the word "groupie" had not yet arrived in the band vernacular. Clare was in total agreement when I suggested we form our own group. I went to Jim Marshall's music shop in Hanwell, and the guitar salesman was more than helpful in setting me on the right track. His name was Terry Slater, and he invited me to come and hear his own band the following weekend.

I invested 28 pounds from my Walls Vanilla Gold account on a secondhand Hofner bass, and another 20 on a Watkins 50-watt amplifier and bass cabinet. Clare and I found a drummer and a lead guitarist, both Irish; we called our group the Teenbeats. We made our first booking three weeks later; it was for a wedding reception at a Scout hall in Greenford. We had been rehearsing every night, and I, no longer at

Walls or going to the Inishfree, was practising every day. We knew eight songs: "Hello Mary Lou" by Rick Nelson, "Sea of Heartbreak" by Don Gibson, "Jailhouse Rock" by Elvis, "Cathy's Clown" by the Everly Brothers, "Johnny B. Goode" by Chuck Berry, "Blueberry Hill" by Fats Domino, and "Sweet Nothin's'" by Brenda Lee. We played each song three times in the set, and we did Elvis' "Hound Dog" twice as the encore. The bride was Irish, so we finished off the proceedings with the Irish National Anthem, which we somehow managed to play and sing in Gaeliga. The groom, who was cockney, kept coming onto the stage and singing with me, shouting into the microphone, "I want to tell my bride how much I fucking love her . . . This one is for you, doll." They must have liked us enough, as we were paid ten pounds each (nearly two weeks' rent for one hour's work!), and we were told to drink and eat as much as we wanted.

Going back to see Terry Slater at Marshall's, I put a down payment on a new P.A. system—this was getting serious now. I got on really well with him, and he did me a few favours over the following weeks. Who was to know that nine years later he would become musical director and lead guitarist for the Everly Brothers, moving with his family to Nashville, USA? I would send him a demo of a song I had written with Chris Thomas called "Finding it Rough" . . . And fuck me, didn't the Everly Brothers eventually release a great version of it! Some years later, when they were on a British tour, Terry would introduce me to Don and Phil; it was still hard to believe that here I was in their dressing room, being thanked for the song by my idols, who I used to listen to on the jukebox in Tramore's Amusement Arcade, where I went for the summer holidays. Talk about fantasy and dreamland!

The Teenbeats, with Clare and I sharing lead vocals, continued to play weddings and other social functions in the Ealing, Hanwell and Greenford areas, but I was also making some moves in other directions. Clare worked full-time as an electrician, and the others also had day jobs—they were not prepared to give them up and devote everything to making music, so I was seeking out new contacts further afield in Brentford, Richmond, Chiswick and Acton, and listening to rhythm & blues and bluebeat with the intention of leaving pronto to form my own group and play the music that obsessed me more and more.

It was nearly Christmastime, and I decided to go to Ireland and tell my parents of my decision to work in the world of music. They were disappointed, but did not stand in my way, for which I am forever grateful. At the end of January, I returned to London and based myself in Ealing Broadway.

Within three months, with my new pal Vic Griffiths from Brentford (a storming blues harmonica player and a tight rhythm guitarist), I had put together a new band called the Second Thoughts; the other three musicians were from the Ealing and Acton areas. I survived by putting on rhythm & blues nights where I booked local town halls, printed posters and handouts, and put on the Second Thoughts as the main attraction of the night; my girlfriend ran the door, and after paying ourselves in the band, rental fee for the hall and printing costs, I often had a profit of over 30 pounds—maybe the streets of London were paved with gold after all! The Second Thoughts became one of West London's best-known groups, and we started to get bookings upwest at places like the 51 Club, and out in the Home Counties. Within a year we were playing on the stage of the legendary Star Club in Hamburg, Germany. I had achieved what

I had hoped and worked for—to be in a good band, to travel and to live the life.

> ***Old town, new town***
> ***Sheepskin coat and leather trousers.***
> ***Black snowflakes falling on white houses and***
> ***Hundreds of butterflies coming out of his mouth.***
> ***Your twist and my shout, How can I get out?***

For a year I forgot who I was, and that's not easy to do if you are born and bred an Irishman, but it was something that had to be done. Then one day I woke up, and I could see myself in the sun.

Indulgent Recommendation for the iPod Generation

The Appletree Theatre, *Playback*, 1968 (Verve)

The Everly Brothers, *Bowling Green*, 1967 (Warner Bros.)

Rick Nelson, *Another Side of Rick*, 1967 (Decca)

HARPS AND PILLS

Ronnie Wood, Pete Townshend, Speedy Keen, John McVie, Robert Stigwood, the Rolling Stones, 1963-66

I slept there, I leapt there
I let my hair grow long there
I dropped there, I stopped there
I lost and found my way there
I was high there, I watched you cry there
I sang the blues all night there
I walked there, I tripped there
I met you at the bus stop there
I played there, I strayed there
I wish that I had prayed there.

I lived all over Ealing in the early to mid-'60s; I moved around with a decadent crowd, a band of urban gypsies who crashed in each other's rooms, bed-sits and flats, or broke into empty houses and stayed till the owners returned with the estate agent who was handling the property.

The Uxbridge Road between Ealing Common and

Hanwell was our highway, and Ealing Broadway was the hub. We only left the area to go up West late on a Friday night to do harps and pills at the all-nighters of the 51 Club in Great Newport Street (also known as Ken Colyer's club) or to the Limbo Club off Berwick Street.

Most of the crowd I moved with were trying to put together a band; some were good blues guitarists, others played a small harmonica, a blues instrument better known as a "harp" or "vamper." As you blew or sucked your way up and down the scale of notes, you could make it sing blue or make it wail like a freight train going to New Orleans; you could slap it with your arched hand and make it gasp like a woman on the cusp of her pleasure; you could rasp and mute it and let it moan, on a holding note, and it was all down to the expertise of your tongue, lips and fingertips. They came in different keys, and if you were good, you could bring the Mississippi Delta to Ealing Broadway. We all carried them around in our pockets, ready for action with a group or a duo who were starting to put things together.

I knew of Sonny Terry and Slim Harpo—brilliant exponents of the blues harp who had made recordings in America that could be purchased in Dobells Import Store in Leicester Square. I heard them for the first time at Eddie Wilkins' flat near Ealing Art School. He was supposed to be doing a graphics course but never went; he had bigger fish to fry with his own lucrative import/export business. He gave me his registration card, which got me free food in the canteen, and I sometimes sneaked into photographic classes and lectures. I became aware of a blues/trad scene going on at the college. A band called the Tridents had a regular lunchtime session. Art Wood, Ronnie's older brother, was doing something with more of a trad-jazz/blues feel, and Pete Townshend and his mate Barney were up to some creative mischief that eventually led to the Detours, the High Numbers and The Who. Pete was an Acton boy, a Mod, and when he met Roger Daltrey and John Entwistle, who both came from Acton, then I only saw him at venues like the Railway Hotel at Harrow or somewhere up West at the weekend. We did have a very close mutual friend, a drummer called John "Speedy" Keen.

The next time I met Pete Townshend was in March 2007, when I was in Los Angeles to promote a Nirvana track for the film *Children of Men*. Martin Lewis, a music/film journalist and a mutual friend of Pete and me, arranged the surprise meeting in Long Beach, where The Who were doing a show that evening. Pete and I had a strange but wonderful time reminiscing those Ealing days over a cuppa. Forty years evaporated in four seconds; it was like walking into the Wimpy Bar at the Broadway to wait for Speedy and Pete Meaden to turn up. Fond memories in abundance. Townshend gave me a feeling of warmth and generosity that comes with being blessed to be alive and healthy and never having lost his enthusiasm for the creative process. As a guitarist, he is naturally gifted; as a songwriter, he is a supreme craftsman, and as a showman, he always made sure that The Who delivered live . . . and that night was no exception. It was truly special.

The cuppa tea was back again during their show, when Roger and Pete closed the set with an acoustic song about that very subject. It was a very clever cooldown, as they enjoyed a cuppa onstage and saluted the Californian audience with typical West London Boy cheers.

Tea is their strongest beverage these days!! I

remembered the last time I saw them live—40 years before, in the bad old good old days of the Railway Hotel out Harrow way; it was a bottle of Southern Comfort they were passing around. But 2007 was the first time I'd heard this recent Townshend song, and all kinds of tea memories came flooding back . . . The ABC Café and the Wimpy Bar opposite each other at Ealing Broadway where we consumed gallons of the stuff . . . Speedy Keen's mum at Hanwell shouting up to the bedroom where we floated like two velvet clouds . . . "Are you and Pat ready for a lovely cuppa, John?" and Speedy's reply, "Can't you see we're fuckin' sleepin', Mother!" He loved his mum and dad dearly, and he spoke in the house the way he spoke on the street; that's how it was, no pretence . . . Don Partridge, the one-man-band busker, spent a lot of his time around the Broadway; he had a number-one chart hit called "Rosie" he wrote and performed around that time.

In Cockney slang, "Rosie Lee" meant "tea"; the way it works is, "tea" rhymes with "Rosie Lee," so you would say, "Fancy a cuppa Rosie?" Another example would be if you were uptown for a curry, you would say, "I'm going for a Ruby." Ruby Murray was a famous singer at that time, and the inventiveness in Cockney rhyme language is in the clever use of the first word, not the rhyme word, to describe the situation or the object.

Martin invited me to Chateau Marmont hotel for a drink after the show. He had arranged to meet up with Ringo's son Zak Starkey, the drummer with The Who. I was feeling melancholic from the day's events—so many flashbacks and feelings—and what I really wanted was to get back to my daughter's place, where I was in temporary residence -- the day had left me full of melancholia.

* * *

John McVie, a bass player from West Ealing, was in a band called the Krewsaders. He was the first to introduce me to Howlin' Wolf and the song "Smokestack Lightning." He lived with his parents right by the Wimpy Bar in West Ealing where a lot of these formative bands used to meet for the purpose of chatting up girls from the local schools and endless music-speak. We used his bedroom, where he had a very good system, to listen to the most recently sourced singles. After hearing "Smokestack Lightning," I abandoned my acoustic guitar and borrowed some money against it, enough to go to Jim Marshall's Music Shop in Hanwell and put down a deposit on a Watkins electric guitar and amplifier with in-built speakers and a Copycat echo unit.

The guitar salesman was a fellow called Terry Slater, and we became good friends. In a way I suppose I saw him as a father figure, adviser, someone reliable on the scene and always ready to give you a chance to make your desire a reality. At night he put together and played lead guitar in backup bands for American acts who were coming over to do the new British tours. I went to see him at Hammersmith on a Little Richard/Jerry Lee Lewis spectacular, and after a few minutes I realised that the drum salesman from Marshall's, Mitch Mitchell, was laying it down on a sparkling red-glitter Ludwig kit. What a transformation. In the shop he was sugar and spice, but onstage he was a man possessed by the beat. They worked in the Hanwell store six days a week and played almost every night, and if they were going up to Liverpool or Manchester, Jim Marshall let them off early afternoon to get on the road in time to make the gig, and they could choose the best of the shop's guitars and drum kits to play and showcase. Maybe that was the answer: Get a job in a guitar shop and have the best of both worlds. Terry liked to play a Gretsch guitar, and a few years later I bought a secondhand one myself, a beautiful shade of olive green; if I had it today, it would be worth a fortune.

Things were beginning to come together for me. I remember going to see Cliff Bennett and the Rebel Rousers at an R&B venue above Burton's in Uxbridge. They played great covers of Coasters songs, and the best version I ever heard of Barrett Strong's "Some Other Guy," one of my all-time favourite songs, also covered by the Beatles and the Big Three from Liverpool. Jimmy Royal and the Hawks were another local band I went to see in Southall and Uxbridge—a slick outfit with a great repertoire of covers.

At John McVie's house one day I met Cliff Barton, a genius bass player who should have been born black. He knew so much about the blues, but he died too young from his addiction. His record collection was the Holy Grail for many of the musicians around Ealing. I knew Tom Newman, a guitarist and singer from Perivale, who had a band called the Tomcats (which became the Cat and later July); nine years on in 1972 he was working on *Tubular Bells* with Mike Oldfield. Frank Kennington, whom I met years later in Los Angeles, where he was a music promoter, and Mickey Lieber, an excellent guitarist, were rehearsing around the Hanger Lane area, and in the middle of it all was John "Speedy" Keen, a drummer with a manic force of energy bar none, who lived in Hanwell. I lived with him and his mum and dad for a few months until we were shown the door by his mum for taking too many liberties. I have to admit our behaviour was well over the top. It all came to a head when we got stoned and started playing two drum kits—a face-off at 4 in the morning after we had barricaded his bedroom door with two mattresses. It brought all the screaming neighbours out on the street, the Law and the Council were called in, and his parents were threatened with eviction; so much for his mum's cuppa, the best I had tasted since I had come over from Ireland.

Speedy became the drummer of the Second Thoughts until he moved on with his own idea a year later, and with the help and production of Pete

Townshend and Kit Lambert, he formed Thunderclap Newman, wrote the classic "Something in the Air" on a broken four-string guitar that he kept in the back of his car, and our paths only crossed over the following years at the Speakeasy Club.

I realised that pills, weed and trips were keeping many of the people I knew in a dark place, and that it was important for me to bring moderation to my own hedonistic, indulgent ways if I was really serious about getting something together. I started the Second Thoughts with Vic "The Dog" Griffiths from South Ealing, the best blues harp and rhythm guitarist in the Ealing area; Speedy was on drums; Mickey Holmes from Northfields, formerly with John McVie in the Krewsaders, was the bass player, later to be replaced by Chris "Tiff" Thomas. The late Tony Duhig from Ealing Common was on lead guitar. I used to see him at the 207 bus stop, carrying a guitar, and one day went up to him and said, "Are you in a band, man?" to which he replied, "Not yet, but I practise every day to T-Bone Walker." That was good enough for me. I invited him to come to a rehearsal the next day, and he turned up with his friend John Field, who played congas and percussion.

By that evening, I had the group I wanted. After the Second Thoughts broke up, Tony and John along with Tom Newman became July, and later they became Jade Warrior when Tom broke up July. It sounds incestuous, and it was.

My blues influences changed weekly as I discovered more new artists to idolise, but Jimmy Reed and Mose Allison were the main ones for me, and as the singer I tried to get as many of their songs as possible into our set list. Vic was big on Chuck Berry and Bo Diddley, and I bought four pairs of maracas to fill out the sound on the covers of songs like "You Can't Judge a Book by Lookin' at the Cover," "Mona," "Roadrunner," "I'm a Man" and a couple of Wilbur Harrison songs. That was the backbone of our show; in no time at all we became the most popular band in the area, playing Scout halls and town halls, putting on our own promotions wherever we could hire an interesting venue. We started to bring in decent money, which allowed me to pay off my debts to Jim Marshall Music Shop and to astonish three different landlords by making good my back rent.

So the Second Thoughts were on a roll, and the only other competition was a band from Hayes called the Birds, which Ron Wood had put together, but Hayes and the Birds were not on my radar until I realised that Woody and I were sleeping with the same girl from Hanger Lane.

The Ealing Jazz and Blues Club at the Broadway was the mecca to play for any band on the up; we were going to get our shot very soon. The club was an important milestone in the group explosion that was happening all over London with acts such as Alexis Korner, Cyril Davies All Stars, Manfred Mann with singer Paul Jones on harp, the Yardbirds with Keith Relf the singer and harpist and Clapton on guitar, Downliners Sect, Long John Baldry, and the hottest act of them all, the Rolling Stones. The Stones had two excellent harpists, Brian Jones and Mick Jagger, with Brian playing bottleneck guitar on many songs, which gave him the authoritative presence of the man in charge of things, at least onstage.

Ferre acted as promoter-manager-booker of the Ealing Club. A sharp, Arabic-looking 30-year-old, he always gave free admittance to the girls he would attempt to harem later that night. He was from Egypt, Lebanon or Morocco, depending on whom you spoke to, but he could be quite English when required. Ferre was straight to the point and on the ball.

If you were the headline act, Ferre paid you a percentage of the door, so the more clubbers you could get down there through word of mouth, the more you got paid. The support bands were not paid at all, but Ferre would give you, depending on his mood or how much he liked your band, petrol expenses and vouchers for breakfast at the ABC Café next door. The Ealing Club, with its long, low arched brick ceilings, was a sweatbox under the railway lines of Ealing Broadway Station; the vibrations of the fast trains into Paddington from the west added another dimension to the rhythms of the driving bass and drums.

When we had a few support slots under our belts, Ferre gave us our very own headlinering night, and from that we were able to graduate to the London R&B circuit proper, playing the Crawdaddy Club at the Station Hotel in Richmond, the Rickytick Club in Windsor, the 51 Club in Great Newport Street, Soho (this was the gig sought after by every band in the London area), and the Klooks Kleek in West Hampstead, where on one memorable night we supported the legendary John Lee Hooker.

That experience was one of trepidation, but also pride and humility to be on the same stage as a man who had really lived the blues and was prepared to share them through his music and through his "smile on whatever" attitude toward life.

At that time in 1964, there were pubs, mostly up North London, Kilburn, Camden Way, and I knew a couple in Shepherd's Bush and Acton that were frequented by local thugs and yobs, so-called "hardmen," always in a gang, inciting others to do their dirty work for them. If they heard an Irish accent or took a dislike to your friendly manner, it was "Why don't you fuck off, Paddy, back to where you came from." Thank God I have always been able to see beyond that kind of ignorance wherever I've gone in the world, an attitude I put down to my education in Ireland, whose people are most tolerant and hospitable despite centuries of oppression.

Our Friday-night residency at the 51 Club brought us to the attention of two management/publicist hippies, Simon Hayes and Ray Williams. They had an office-flat-den-crash-pad in one of the side streets leading off the Kings Road in Chelsea and had worked the single "I Got You Babe" by Sonny and Cher, but most important, they had an in with Robert Stigwood, or "Stiggy" as they called him, and for about three months we felt they were going to take the Second Thoughts to the same dizzy heights where Stiggy reigned among the royalty of music entrepreneurs.

They hired a recording studio somewhere in the depths of Wimbledon, and we did two songs—the Wilbur Harrison classic "Let's Get Together" and a new song we had introduced to our set, T.J. Arnall's "Cocaine," which I had heard Davy Graham play live at a club in Chelsea. I do not recall very much about those three months with Simon and Ray; if I try to go there, it is full of ghosts, spacers, and time tarnished but not wasted. I do remember Simon giving me a heavy piece of thick 7-inch vinyl with a white label, on which he had printed "2nd Thoughts," which really pissed me off because of the "Second" being replaced by the numeral. After hearing it a few times, I decided it was a piece of shit and threw it to the floor, where it smashed into pieces. I did change my mind, however, when in the early '90s I was doing a guest DJ spot on New York's Radio NYU for a psychedelic-rock phone-in show, where I got to play anything of my own choice over a two-hour time slot, chatting to the programme's resident host, "The Paisley Piper." I had briefly mentioned the Second Thoughts in the interview part, and to my amazement we had a caller from New Jersey who said he had a copy of the single. Fucking hell, I thought. Who are these people, aliens? We spoke live on air, and he had all of the recordings I had made over the years. He came into New York the following day and brought me a cassette copy, and when I heard it, I was lost for words—I thought it was brilliant! The Second Thoughts' version of "Let's Get Together" had that right dirty edge of R&B originality that Bryan Ferry's pop hit version lacked. Coincidentally, Ferry's was produced by our old bass player, Chris "Tiff" Thomas, who had gone on to desk duty at the EMI George Martin School of Excellence and become a much sought-after producer whose credits include Procol Harum, the Sex Pistols, the Pretenders, Bryan Ferry, the Climax Blues Band and the Beach Boys; he also worked on the Beatles' *White Album, and did mix work on Pink Floyd's Dark Side of the Moon*.

Back at Ealing Broadway, everyone was spaced; in fact, it seemed to me that the whole of London's

population was out there somewhere. Simon and Ray kept saying, "We will fix a meeting with Stiggy." We were offered a month's contract to go to Hamburg and Frankfurt; we would leave in two weeks, in our own transit van, for which we would be reimbursed expenses, but first we had a sharing headliner with the Rolling Stones at the Ealing Club. It was to be their farewell gig—as there were so many people following them, the club was too small for Ferre to book them again. They were on their way to the big time, and everybody knew it. I can still hear the music they played that night; it was possessed, driven, wild, and its naked force of energy just took over. I have never heard another live act come close to what they gave that night. We had played a good set before they came on, but it was stiff with internal conflict and uncertainty—I knew what we could generate when we were really playing together as a solid unit. I remember thinking we were the local band turning up to be blown away by a band about to go global. They ripped their way through "I'm a King Bee," "Carol," "Poison Ivy," "Route 66," "I'm a Man," "Cops and Robbers," "Diddly Daddy" . . .

The Stones were the best rhythm & blues/rock and roll band I have ever heard, to this day—Keith driving his riffs like a jackhammer; Brian sliding on his trusted Gretsch and vamping on his harps; Charlie and Bill laying down the solid foundations; Ian Stewart, their roadie and minder, playing left-hand boogie on a battered upright piano, his right hand seeming always busy manipulating a porkpie or a sandwich towards his mouth; and "Mick the Lip" in his element, showmanship personified, playing harmonica to make you swear Jimmy Reed was onstage. He could have had any girl in the room that night; he'd probably already had a number of them anyhow.

There was very little interaction between the Stones—just a look and a nod every so often. Theirs was a special understanding, honed by being together

24 hours a day, living, playing, sharing the subtle mix of the straight and dangerous that each one brought to the Stones. They made their own star quality, and they were a sweet and tight playing machine.

When it was over, both bands had to get their gear out and up the 30 steps to street level and onto the waiting Ford transits. We were going on to do an all-nighter at 51 Club in Leicester Square, sharing the bill with the Downliners Sect, and the Stones were driving overnight to Liverpool.

Everyone leaving the club was soaked in sweat; the walls dripped with condensation. But there was another gig to get to, a chance for our band to put on a better show for our fans, who were now on their way to Central London by tube from Ealing Broadway Station. Before we departed, I went quickly to the men's at the end of the club—a small, smelly box with no washbasin, but Ferre had drilled tiny holes in a surrounding waist-high pipeline that flushed where you took a leak, so you were able to splash water on your face and hands with the tiny water jets that shot from it. While I was doing my splash-up, Mick Jagger came in carrying a handmade wooden box that contained all the harps that he and Brian had used onstage—about twenty in total, all in different keys—and proceeded to wash them individually and dry them off with a small towel. "What's all that about?" I asked him. "Brian says it's my fucking job, man. I do it after every gig." "Is Brian running the band?" I asked him curiously. He looked at me with one of his typical cynical grins. "No fucking way, man. Ian is the chief! No one messes with him, not even Brian."

The next time I saw Mick was backstage at the concert in Hyde Park on July 5th, 1969, two days after Brian had drowned in the swimming pool of his home at Hartfield in Sussex, a shocking and mysterious tragedy that still leaves many questions unanswered . . . When you light a firework, always make sure you stand well back.

Indulgent Recommendation for the iPod Generation

Jimmy Reed, *Sun Is Shining* (Snapper compilation)

Jimmy Reed, *Jimmy Reed at Carnegie Hall* , 1961 (Vee-Jay)

THE ST. JOHN'S WOOD AFFAIR

I knew Silent Derek would be there, and Suzy with her gay pals the Trinity—Sean and Eric were twins, so fuck knows why they called themselves the Trinity; weird is not the word.

Pete the Pencil was a permanent fixture. He was the landlord's nephew. He came close to my face and said, "Have some munchies, man, wonderful stuff, just out of the oven and ready to warm your brain." Taffy spoke: "It's mellow, man, fucking real mellow." Five minutes? Five hours? It was hard to tell, and easy to forget how long I was posturing there on the sofa-bed, trying to find something tangible to think about, to focus on. I was at the edge of something that felt like paranoia. I could see myself looking at me—illusion or delusion? And the others, what were they looking at? Maybe I was stoned? No fucking way, man! I had tried before, and I could never really get out of it for real. "You been buying the wrong kind of shit, man," Taffy always smirked.

The munchie party was in full floating mode. Derek, Suzy, the Trinity, Pencil—all swimming in their own wave. With Taffy one never knew whether he was swimming or drowning. "Stay cool, baby, you're sound," the Pencil said. "I love you too," Suzy mouthed back. "I'd love you more if you passed me the wafers." Taffy had meant to say papers . . . or did he? I knew I could hear Charles Mingus blasting out "Oh Lord, Don't Let Them Drop That Atomic Bomb on Me" from the speaker next to Taffy, who was putting on the sounds.

I started to focus my attention towards a bookshelf over Pencil's shoulder. Hockney, Kandinsky, Nabokov, Henry Miller, Dali, *Lord of the Flies, Lord of the Rings* and *Winnie the Fucking Pooh.* I started to get the giggles; tears rolled down my cheeks. I was laughing in my own crying; maybe this time I was stoned! Not a hope in the fires of hell. Then straight out of Munchieland it came to me . . . an overpowering desire to eat cherries. I could taste the juice in my mouth; it was all over my hands. An invasion of cherries avalanched through the door of the room, and the red wave washed all over me. I could hear Mingus playing cherry shapes on the double bass. Another book on the shelf grabbed my attention: *The Cherry Orchard*. "Was that a Russian cunt?" I heard myself say to Taffy, knowing that the nature of the beast in him would give flight to his nationalistic feelings and he would throw me another of his one-liners. "Fucking hell, man, no, it was a Welsh cunt from Cardigan Bay."

Suzy the model flower-child nymph was now naked and dancing horizontal to my vertical. She started pissing on my legs, moving around the room wailing like a demented banshee. She pissed all over Pencil and the Trinity, who found it absolutely hilarious. As she came by Taffy, he smacked her cherub arse with the Mingus LP cover and she let out a kittenish cry . . . Was I stoned? No fucking way, kiddo . . . but I was wet.

The Trinity threw their clothes off and joined in the free-spirit dancing with Suzy, making tribal moves as they chanted, "Come on, baptise us again, Suzeeee." Taffy put Howlin' Wolf's "Smokestack Lightning" on the player; a cyclonic wedge of rhythm & blues thundered down from the 12-inch speaker cabinet, which was set on slabs of pavement stone seconded from the street outside, and so it went on to its inevitable crashed-out destination . . . oh yeah!!

As the first light came up, I found myself counting the slates on the church roof across the street. The flat was on the fourth floor and had a bay window that overlooked most of St. John's Wood. I counted each one as if it was the most important slate on the roof. I had been to a few crash pads before, but this one had a strange, uncomfortable denial about it; I wanted to get out of there, now, back to West London and into a bath of perfumed soap bubbles.

Silent Derek was watching me through half-closed eyes as I tried to find my jacket and boots. The only sound in the room as I quietly left was the hypnotic circular scratching of the stylus needle, which was still sitting on a revolving LP. At the bottom, in the entrance hall, I could hear foreign voices from behind a door. I stopped momentarily to listen, and in doing so missed the last steps and went straight down, my face kissing the concrete, my boots and jacket joining me in the arena of contact. The flat door opened at the commotion. Two teenage beauties appeared to find me on my arse, blood pouring down my face.

I was not sure if I could get up. I was disoriented, but felt no pain as the foreign fragrant bodies on either side of my pissed-on person helped me into their flat, where they proceeded to clean me up with great attention and detail. They insisted I take a bath while they put my bloodstained clothes in the washing machine.

They cooked a breakfast, and I stayed there for three days of hedonistic indulgence, to which they were instigators and I was a more than willing participant. They told me about some of their London adventures, including a wild party they went to after meeting Viv Prince, the drummer of the Pretty Things, and Dave Davies of the Kinks in the Ship pub in Wardour Street, Soho. I knew Viv Prince and the antics he could get up to, so I thought, "In for a penny, in for a pound." We slept together, we messed around together, we got bevvied up in the night and listened to the music and they danced together, and in the afternoons they went to their English-language class in Tottenham Court Road from 3 to 6. On the Wednesday, they returned to Denmark and I went back to Ealing. They were living in Copenhagen with their parents, who were bakers and had their own konfitori—a cake and coffee house.

I met up with one of them—the other sister had got married—when Nirvana toured Scandinavia five years later to promote the single "Rainbow Chaser"; it had reached number one in the Danish charts. The Danes have very good taste and style. Their cakes are wonderful, the beer is special. And they gave me my first experience of a threesome . . . and a hit single.

Indulgent Recommendation for the iPod Generation

Charles Mingus, *Oh Yeah*, 1962 (Atlantic)

Recommended tracks:

Oh Lord, Don't Let Them Drop That Atomic Bomb on Me

Eat That Chicken

Passions of a Man

(Roland Kirk played on the sessions.)

Pete Meaden

OOOPS

Playing the American Bases, Jimmy James, Pete Meaden, 1965

The American Air Force bases in Oxfordshire were a hidden source of electric and eclectic musical inspiration to many of the good groups around the West London music scene in the early '60s. By military transport, the Americans brought over blues and soul outfits out of New York, Chicago and Detroit to entertain their troops at Brize Norton. Every two weeks, usually on a Saturday, there was a show, and they booked London R&B groups to support the main acts of the night. It was a great opportunity for the Second Thoughts, the Mark Leeman 5, the Tridents, James Royal and the Hawks, Frankie Reid and the Casuals, and others to play at such unusual and full-on venues. I had made a contact at the Flamingo Club in Wardour Street, who put me in touch with the man at the Base. My contact was one of the many American soldiers who came to the Flamingo for the live music all-nighters and other pleasures of that street when they were off duty and had managed to secure a weekend pass.

The American bands and solo artists were nearly always black, as were many of the soldiers on the base; their music was the real deal, while the London groups were all white boys searching for and sometimes finding the blues. We in the Second Thoughts supported Percy Sledge and John Lee Hooker on the bases, and shared a billing with Jimmy James & the Vagabonds.

Local girls from the towns and villages in the vicinity made their own way, or could be shuttled in by military transport for the weekend dance. The girls always looked the business—hair up in the beehive style, Brigitte Bardot poutiness and cleavage, flashing bare skin above the nylon stockings and suspenders as their skirts swirled, jiving, spinning legs of temptation in white stilettos . . . maybe later in the wee wee hours giving some lucky fella a good seeing-to. We always went down early, as a meal was included in the booking arrangement of the band, just like a rider that bands many years later insisted on. The soldiers and staff made you feel very much at home in their tiny independent state in the centre of rural England. They had their own schools, shops, church and hospital—a self-sufficient unit of men and women, many of them ready to be called into action at any time.

These show nights often attracted over 600 people; the booze was dirt cheap. it was not a place for radical or racial viewpoint; there was never any antagonism or aggressive behaviour. It was all about music, dancing and worship of the opposite sex, having a ball and letting your hair down—the hair thing only applied literally to the girls and the London R&B bands (who already had hair down on our shoulders), as the American men's heads were shaved or crew-cut.

In the mess halls and canteens, they had jukeboxes with some known, unknown and difficult-to-find 45rpm singles from the gospel, rhythm & blues, rock and roll, and jazz labels in the States. There was a thriving business on the base for these black-market nuggets and for American Air Force clothes—the brown leather bomber-pilot jackets were especially desired, as were baseball caps and original Levi's. The more people that you got to know at the base and in the Flamingo, the cheaper the price became. I still have a Jerry Butler single, "He Will Break your Heart" from the Vee-Jay label, and a Sam Cooke and Soul Stirrers gospel album, from that time and place. I paid five shillings for both; that's 25 pence in today's currency. The Jerry Butler song reminds me of someone I met one Saturday at the base in Brize Norton.

As we did our show that night, I saw a pretty, buxom girl dancing with another girl near the stage. When we had finished, I went to the bar, and they were both there. I bought them a drink; the one I liked was drinking cider, and her friend was on "snowballs"—advocat (eggnog) and lemonade. They were both from Banbury, with their strong local accent; I just about understood their lingo amid the giggling and feigned shyness, and they were not dancing on the slow numbers. I started to chat up the one I fancied.

Her name was Rita, and when I was up close to her, she looked as if she could suck me in and blow me out in bubbles; she was a big girl. They came to all the "hops"—that's the word they used—they loved dancing, and from the way they led each other into the moves, you knew they were best friends from when they were at school. The dance hall—in fact it might have been one of the hangars—was dimly lit, but there was a revolving mirror ball that had the effect of making everyone look special; it added an air of mystery and excitement to the proceedings. You felt that you could take a few liberties in there, like putting your hand under a girl's skirt while you were dancing. Rita and I danced the slows, which was one in every four dances, while her friend sipped her snowball, and then the two partnered up again.

We fancied each other—French kissing, wandering hands sending messages. It looked very promising, and a window of opportunity certainly existed for us. The Second Thoughts were booked to play there again on the following Saturday; Rita and I made a very definite date to meet again. When I left the bar to go and get our money and put our gear away in the van, she tongued and whispered in my ear, "I like you."

Come the day one week later, expectation was high for the date with Rita, and the band had a buzz to be playing there again. There were two bands on before us; from the side of the stage I looked a few times to see if Rita and her friend were anywhere near the front, but I could not see them—the place was packed to the rafters. We put on a good show and really got the crowd going, finishing our set with three Bo Diddley numbers linked together: "Mona," "I'm a Roadrunner" and "You Can't Judge a Book by the Cover." I had three pairs of maracas in each hand, for laying down that hypnotic shuffle made famous by Bo, Jerome and the Duchess, and when we hit the final chord, as the snare drum smashed behind me, I threw the lot into the crowd—they went spare, 12 maracas flying through the air never to be seen again! I had to go to Marshall's in Hanwell on the Monday and buy a load of new ones.

I was on a definite high when I made it to the bar on the lookout for Rita. It was a slow number; I saw her friend at the bar but no Rita. I moved around the perimeter of the dance area as the mirror ball tossed its silver reflections into the crowd. I was peering in amongst the shapes and sizes when I spotted her, hanging like a sleepy puppy, her arms around the neck of the singer from the band that was on before us—they were all over each other. I walked in to where they were, and as they continued dancing, if that is what you could call it, I tapped her on the arm. She opened her eyes and looked at me with innocent amazement. "What's going on?" I said. "I thought we had a date." Over his shoulder she mouthed to me, like a ventriloquist's dummy, pointing at the back of his head with just a hint of indecision on her face . . . "I thought it was you." He never turned around, but I could see his hair was long and curly like mine; he had a velvet jacket on, so did I.

I walked off the dance floor, went outside and smoked a joint with our harmonica player. I came back to the bar and asked Snowball if she would dance a slow . . . and we did.

There were three reggae/soul-influenced bands around at that time in the London region who played the bases—Gino Washington and the Ram Jam Band, Jimmy James and the Vagabonds, and Herbie Goins and the Night Timers. Whenever I saw them, there was always a smart, Ivy League, Mod-looking early-20s dude with them. I thought he was the manager of all three bands. This turned out to be Peter Meaden. When I met Pete in 1963, he straightened me out on who was who and what was what. One of the first things he said to me, right at the beginning of our friendship, was, "I am going to set up my own publicity, promotion, management and record-production company, and it is going to be called "Ooops." He gave me a business card with just the word "Ooops" printed in the centre—no telephone number for contact, not even his name. I thought it was genius; he was a fucking brilliant guy and he didn't know it.

I felt he was one of those rare characters who preferred to fuck up rather than follow someone's rule book. The more time I spent with him, the more I realised he was dynamite waiting to be fused, creativity constantly enthused, ideas instantly transfused, every whimsical moment confused, outrageous and flirtatious when amused, his faith and trust in some, abused; he was often misconstrued but never needed to be excused. He was persuasive, as he showed with the The Who in summer of 1964, when he put together a promotion of calculated ideas to relaunch them as the High Numbers with the Mod gear and Union Jack fashion regalia. He also wrote their single release "I'm the Face" C/W "Zoot Suit" before they went back to being The Who. Was Meaden their manager? Did he have some sort of contract? I don't think he was bothered about that aspect of the relationship, but it did take some "front and flannel" to be able to get difficult Pete, explosive Roger, unpredictable Moonie and stubborn John to change their name and drape themselves in the flag of Britannia. No wonder they started to smash their gear onstage, and then found that the audiences loved it. However, I don't think it mattered one iota what they were called: The Who, the High Numbers, the Acton Boys, whatever! The combination of those four musicians and their talents was always going to be a winning formula, as they proved with their worldwide success and longevity.

Pete Meaden and I got on famously right from the off. We did a real mix of clubland when we went out to play. We were speed personified, from Le Kilt to La Poubelle, French clubs in Soho that were home to students and au pairs from Europe. And there was Le Duce, a gay Mod club that became the scene a few years later just as homosexuality became legal in 1967 . . . but you did not have to be gay or a Mod to be admitted there, or to Jack's, a private bar near the Marquee music venue in Wardour Street, which attracted journalists and writers, members only, allowed to invite one guest. Pete was a member and used the place as his own, for meetings with "the establishment," as he called them. He took me to the Paddington/Edgeware Road area late one night and introduced me to my first experience of a shebeen, an unlicensed drinking club with continual music (ska, reggae and soul) and "dancing dirty." It was in the basement of someone's house; you had to pay to get in, but it was just like a private party. Pete seemed to know everybody there, and his exuberance was infectious. We were the only two white people in the room. I found out later that the organisers moved the shebeens around, and if they suspected a police raid on one that was doing good business, they shut it down for a few weeks and then reopened to even more demand, or they just paid someone off . . . And always the music, the sounds, the tunes, the tracks, music for modernists, for "soul boys," for "rude boys," the trendsetters, the purists, the Sue record label, rhythm & blues, and handmade shoes, expensive suits, Prince Buster, Desmond Dekker, the Miracles, Martha and the Vandellas, eyeshadow, lipstick blush, crossover here, bend over there, the Supremes, Dusty Springfield, amphetamines and barbiturates, weed and speed. A kaleidoscopic hybrid! I never could have imagined Pete on a scooter or wearing a parka; he was a stylist, a real Mod guru, not a goon on a Vespa, though he did say later that *Quadrophenia* was his story, in the sense that he identified with the character at the core of the movie's plot, Jimmy Cooper.

Pete Meaden was close to Pete Townshend over many years, and I can imagine him doing his dialogue like there was no tomorrow and Townshend connecting even quicker. If you were in Pete Meaden's company, it was like dancing in a fountain of ideas . . . and making a movie is the process of dressing up some good ideas. Pete Townshend has always acknowledged Pete Meaden's contribution to the film *Quadrophenia* and its conception, and that is totally in order.

Making music can control you! Your heartbeat is its rhythm! You breathe it day and night; you live in it and it lives in you, a two-way relationship that is unconditional. From my own experience, I would say songwriting is best described as having a divine connection to an unforgiving muse. Pete Meaden knew how to tap into that source; he made the connection.

He was not a musician, but he was an artist in his own right.

Meaden had a lovely girlfriend; they lived together, and it was solid. She gave him the space to fly, and he always came home. I met her a couple of times when the Second Thoughts played around Ealing, and in her company he was exactly the same luminous, humorous bundle of ideas, affectionate and caring to her. He wanted to manage us, and offered to get us on a tour, which sounded very exciting until he told me a few days later that it was four nights around the Isle of Wight, playing the town halls in Sandown, Ryde, Ventnor and Newport. We would share the bill with Jimmy James and the Vagabonds, and our accommodation would be local bed-and-breakfast. He would pay all the expenses. Only Pete could have come up with such a trailblazin' idea. No one toured the Isle of Wight—a tiny, sparsely populated island four miles off the southern coast, opposite Portsmouth—unless you were in a caravan on your summer holidays and over 60! This was seven years before the legendary Isle of Wight Festival of 1970 with Jimi Hendrix, and five years before the first ever Isle of Wight Festival with Jefferson Airplane on the last weekend of August in 1968. I flew in for that happening in all my psychedelic gear and glory, to Hell's Field between Newport and Ventnor.

We accepted Pete's offer, and it was a memorable experience. Jimmy James, Count "Prince" Miller (his co-vocalist), the Vagabonds, the Second Thoughts and Pete arrived off the car ferry into a world of sleepy villages with fuchsia hedgerow that made the narrow roads pleasing to the eye. Everyone was up for it, and our days were more than magical. We went searching for dinosaur fossils and found ley lines near Godshill; there was some weird shit going on down there, I tell you! Hell's Field, Godshill—testing space rockets and submarines, plus a youth subculture, each of its own volition and vitality. The gigs were amazing: The young people seemed to arrive out of nowhere. One minute it was an empty hall, and then it was packed. It was summertime, and we started real late, as they have always done on the continent at the town and village fiestas. Pete was on the door, taking the readies at each venue. I realised that he had organised and promoted the tour on his own. He must have gone there earlier in the year to book the halls and pay a deposit, then had colourful psychedelic posters and flyers printed up and distributed, taking the risk that people would come.

I knew what he was charging to get in, and the takings for the four nights would just about give him a break-even situation against his total expenses. The bands never had to put a hand in their pockets once during the tour; he picked up every tab. Nobody had made money, but it had paid for itself, and it was a wonderful four days . . . *Alice in Wonderland* time.

The Second Thoughts folded, and Ealing became a different place for me. I had set my sights farther afield, and I did not see Pete Meaden again until 1969. His vibrancy was still there, but lost in his own lack of focus. In 1968 he had brought Captain Beefheart and the Magic Band over from the West Coast of America to do a tour in England, but they were detained at Heathrow Airport in all their psychedelic regalia and weirdness. They had no money or work permits, and Pete was grilled by Immigration and the police about his part in the so-called tour. No permission was given for them to play in London, so Amsterdam, with its more flexible entry to perform music at a live venue for a limited stay, was where they found themselves, without Pete.

The band's American record company had pulled some strokes with officialdom. Pete was offloaded instantly, and the Captain and his band were moved on. What a trip, Artie Ripp!

When I now play the classic Captain Beefheart LP of that time, *Trout Mask Replica*, I am with Pete in the chaos of Heathrow. I can hear him cajoling; I know that it is all with heart. All he ever wanted was to share a musical experience with others.

In the spirit of that time in the '60s, the memories I have now of friendship and sharing with certain people do not recede into the past; they proceed with me into the future as if part of my DNA. The only downside is that many of these special characters paid the ultimate price for their uniqueness. Peter Meaden died when he was 37 years young.

Indulgent Recommendation for the iPod Generation

P.F. Sloan, *Sins of a Family*

Captain Beefheart, *Trout Mask Replica*

Herbie Goins, *No. 1 in Your Heart*

A BAND CALLED NIRVANA

Hamburg, Stockholm, Eddie Kassner, the Everly Brothers, Chris Thomas, Alex Spyropoulos, Island Records, 1967

We are a tribe of two, Nirvana is our road. The stars that fall around us are the mysteries that unfold.

During the spring of 1965, I returned to London with a serious chest infection, the result of a decadent bohemian lifestyle in the clublands of Hamburg, Munich, Amsterdam, and the unforgiving coldness and snowstorms of Stockholm. After the Second Thoughts had broken up for the second time, I found myself with a band called Lucifer and the Angels, who were from Sweden. I was serving my apprenticeship as vocalist/

rhythm guitarist with residency stints at the Star Club and the Paradiso, legendary venues of beat music and kingdoms of madness, in Hamburg and Amsterdam.

I abused my body for kicks and made up for my cloistered years with the priests and Christian Brothers of Ireland, as often as I could in a day, in as many perverted and debauched situations as I could discover, and believe me there was a lot to discover in the Reeperbahn St. Pauli area of Hamburg, a street with a notorious reputation for its live sex shows. The Star Club was at the hub of it all. The musicians and the girls hung out together in the bars when they were in between shows, sharing life on the the dark side and often sharing love on the outside. The Star Club put on the best acts from the USA and England. I remember we shared the bill one week with Duane Eddy, Cliff Bennett and the Rebel Rousers, Chris Barber's trad band, and the Big Three from Liverpool. The Beatles and the Searchers crafted and perfected their songs and stage shows during a number of residencies at this 12-hour, nonstop jump joint during the early '60s, as did many other up-and-coming British groups.

I met a girl from Stockholm who had come on an

assignment as a music writer with a pop magazine. She introduced me to a new scene in the Gamlastan area of her home city, where I joined a local band called the Merrymen, but really I had gone there to have an adventure with her. I don't remember much about the music other than the fact that at every show we played, a different American Vietnam draft dodger (mostly black guys) would jump onstage to play bongo drums, sing anti-war songs or read poems. One of them, Teddy from San Diego, told me Sweden was the best place in the world to be if you were on the run from your own country, because you were a pacifist and totally opposed to war." We became friendly, and I kept in touch with him for a couple of years. Then he moved to Japan, and we lost contact.

After four months' hospital treatment, I was put on the road to health by the drug streptomycin; recuperation and proper food did the rest. I was ready again to get back into music, but this time with a different, creative direction. Being back in London for recovery gave me the space to have a good reality check.

I decided no more rhythm & blues bands, no

more endless roads in cold transit vans, no more all-night cafés for egg, burger and chips. I decided to start writing my own songs and recording them onto a Revox tape machine. The Revox 2-track (but you could build more tracks by "bouncing" and "layering") became my best friend. What a wonderful piece of equipment it was for aspiring songwriters. I loved that machine; it was my lifeline to a future in music.

It had taken me six months to recover, and I felt I was ready for the challenge I had set myself. In September I met up with Chris "Tiff" Thomas at his parents' house in Ealing, where he was living rent-free until he could sort himself out. We wrote two songs together and recorded them on the Revox.

In the Second Thoughts, Tiff had been a driving force on bass, but he also played good guitar and piano, and with a drumbeat improvised on a cardboard box and cushion, we had a readymade setup to record an atmospheric, quality demo of the two songs.

We took the demo to the Eddie Kassner Publishing House in Denmark Street, London W1, where Ed and his "honky" Roger Bolton raved about it, signed us as songwriters, paid us a small advance against future royalties, and agreed to exploit the copyrights on our behalf. "Exploit" is a wonderful word if you are a publisher. In the life of the song, which is forever, they and their children and their children thereafter make use of its earnings by owning it in perpetuity, 100 percent, and pay back to the songwriter whatever percentage they screwed you into signing on that first day, or never pay you.

Like so many others during those years, we were naïve about our business, because we could only hear the music; getting the song played on the radio was all we strived for . . . initially! We were in Tin Pan Alley, and I was on the way to Nirvana. One of the songs, "Finding It Rough," on which Tiff had played a dazzling guitar riff, was recorded by the Everly Brothers for their *Bowling Green* LP, released worldwide on Warner USA about two years later. The other song, "Chance for Romance," we recorded as a single ourselves for President Records, Kassner's record company, under the name Hat and Tie. They paid for the recording costs at the famous Regent Sound across the street, which was cheap and had a distinctively dirty sound. Tiff was the Hat of the duo, but does not take kindly to being reminded of it (so I heard), and does not include it in his biographical history . . . Maybe I should add it to his Wikipedia profile.

As the "tie" of the outfit (pun very much intended), I look back with the smile if not the bank account of a multimillionaire, and no regrets, even though Kassner and his son David never paid me a penny in over 40 years on "Finding it Rough," or even sent me a royalty statement.

But the song made a special connection for me. When I was a 15-year-old boy, my family took summer holiday at Tramore County Waterford. Though it had one of the best beaches in the world, all I looked forward to was slipping away up to the Atlantic ballroom and arcade area, where you could play the machines or hang out around the massive Rockola jukebox, into which I pumped by pocket money, endlessly playing "Lipstick on Your Collar" by Connie Francis and "Cathy's Clown" by the Everlys.

That record by Don and Phil was a piece of pure magic. It transported me out of Tramore, out across the Atlantic Ocean, which was just down at the end of the street, straight into the American Dream. I used to sing a third harmony part with Don and Phil, pressing repeat play on the Rockola until one of the floor staff who doubled as bouncers at night told me, "Feck off out of it, you little squirt, and let someone else put money in there."

Songwriting, especially the lyrics, was something I took to very easily, and having secured a cover with "Finding it Rough" by an act I idolised was the highest accolade, beyond my craziest dreams. I felt I had made it before I even started. Money cannot buy that kind of experience.

I have encountered many people in the music business. On the one hand there have been the creative artists, songwriters, musicians, singers. On the other hand there have been the vultures, the piranha, the untalented, the merchants . . . those that I met and worked for at certain times and who had money. I have found them to be totally paranoid, full of bullshit, and fucked up in their personal lives.

"Money is the root of all evil." The more you have, the more greed eats into you, and then you want even more. Success is not in the bank, it is in the heart, and those people that I am talking of here do not have heart. Possibly they saw me as one among many who were deluded with the artistic and creative pursuit of whatever talent we possessed, but don't tell me, as one song publisher did during a social gathering a few years later, "You will never make it, because you don't have any of the three necessary ingredients." I was curious and asked what he meant. He replied, "You're not black, you're not Jewish" (which he was), "and you're not gay." I was stunned just for a moment, and I realised that he was serious, even though we were in a jovial atmosphere and the conversation was light. So my reply, swift and sweet, was, "The best thing I can do, then, is marry your daughter. Do you have any?" He was not amused.

A diverse group of songwriters, session musicians, groupies and roadies frequented a café in Denmark Street (London's Tin Pan Alley) called La Gioconda—everybody knew it as "the Gio." It became my second home, as it did for other songwriters and musicians from Liverpool, Belfast, Wales and the London suburbs. Chris Thomas was not on the scene anymore, because a letter he had written to producer George Martin at EMI Studios in St. Johns Wood (instigated by his parents, who would have preferred him to join the bank), came up trumps. A short while after he wrote the letter asking to be taken on as a pupil/assistant—everything was very formal at EMI, and still is—he showed me the "not just right now" rejection. That was during our experimental songwriting period after the group days. A year later he got the call, and within days was assisting George Martin on Beatles recordings. He had hit the jackpot, and to think that a few years earlier he was a Latimer schoolboy standing in the audience at Ealing Town Hall, where the Second Thoughts regularly played, waiting after the gig to tell me discreetly that he had heard Mickey Holmes, our bass player, was having ultimatum problems with his fiancée—the Group or herself. Tiff told me he knew all our songs, had learned the bass parts, and played a red Fender bass. He got the job, and I hope Mickey Holmes had a happy married life.

Tiff genuinely deserves his international success, for two simple reasons: He is more musically talented on bass, keyboards and maybe even guitar than most of the artists and bands he has produced, and he learned the art of production from a master.

Back at La Gioconda, I had found a cheap place to eat or have endless coffees, mixing with the West

End Wide Boys, film students from St. Martins Art School across in Tottenham Court road, and groupies in black duffle coats and blonde peroxide hair who fell in and out of love with a different musician every week, or sometimes every day. It had the atmosphere of a never-ending all-day party, and you could go on the slate there—pay when you got a gig. What more could you ask for?

In that Limbo land I met Alex (Giorgiou) Spyropoulos. I came in one day in the summer of '66. Dave Preston, John Banks and Johnny Gustaffson from the Merseybeats, a Liverpool band, were just inside the door. There was a space at their table, and I was about to sit there when I heard my name thrown above the vibrant ambience. I took a good gander around; Alex Harvey from Scotland was at a table with two girls I knew from the clothes shop Lord John in Carnaby Street, but beyond them at a far end table I could see "Honky" Roger from Kassner's waving at me to come down. The tables in the Gio had fairly high alcove-type benches on either side, so you sometimes could not see who was being loud or who was hiding away. I could make out in the midst of the action that Lesley Duncan, a class girl singer much in demand by songwriters to "session" their songs, sat at the table next to Roger; the other two were Alex Spyropoulos and his writing partner, Ray Singer (no relation to the sewing machine). Like Tiff and myself, they had also signed to Kassner's, as had Eddie Grant and his Equals, who sat at the next table demanding of Roger to get them on *Top of the Pox* next week for their single "Baby Get Back." (Bands slagged it off, but they all wanted to be on it.) He did get them on, and the song reached Number 1 . . . a smash for Kassner. Roger introduced me to Alex, Ray and Lesley; an instant rapport with Alex was there for all to see.

Alex was from Athens, Greece, and had spent a year in Paris to study law. (His father was a maritime lawyer.) But instead of law, Alex studied French girls and bebop. He had to leave Paris, but could not or did not want to show his face back home, so opted for London. He enrolled at St. Martins, where he met Ray, and together they made a student short film from a script by Ray, for which they had written some songs. On the strength of those songs, they had got their deal with Kassner. Even though they collaborated, their partnership had a painful uneasiness about it. Alex was not comfortable in his skin, and to create some lightness in his being there at all, he flirted continuously with Lesley, much to the amusement of Roger, who called everyone "my boys."

The past is history; the future is a mystery. Today is a gift. That is why it is called the "present."

--old Irish saying

And so the stars in the constellation moved a little; the Greek and the Celt had an unwritten, unexplainable, unconditional awareness and understanding of what was going down, and the first group ever in the world to be called Nirvana was born that day in that café. The bond and the band are still in our lives, 40 years later.

We borrowed some money, and within a few weeks both of us had secured our release from the Kassner straitjacket and started writing new songs together, songs that came from a special place. We became as one person, with a very strong focus, and we had a lot of laughs doing whatever we did—work or play. "Busy man" Ray Singer was still around but just on the peripheral. Whereas we had only one thing going on, he was here, there and everywhere like a blue-arsed fly. If we had written one song, he had written five, and he wanted desperately to be in a band with us.

We started rehearsals with the original lineup of the group, working out new songs; we felt we had five good ones including one we had co-written with Ray. Its development had spanned over the weeks we had first met; it was called "Tiny Goddess," a song Françoise Hardy recorded a few years later in French, German and English—clever girl and beautiful! She was the sweetheart of the Parisienne pop scene at that time. The other four songs were: "Rainbow Chaser," which became our classic Nirvana tune, the first pop record to have phasing on it; "Pentecost Hotel," a European psychedelic single, which was never off the radio playlist of that time and was featured on John Peel's show *The Perfumed Garden* on Radio London (pirate), and again when he went to his Radio 1 BBC shows; "I Believe in Magic," covered in 2007 by the American group Father Blooby from the Miami area; and "We Can Help You," covered by the Alan Bown Set, an English band popular in the mid-'60s. We knew we had something goin' on, and Alex and I had a concept that we shared.

The original Nirvana lineup included Alex (piano, Mellotron and vocals); Brian Henderson (bass) from

Bermuda, found through a *Melody Maker* advert; Sylvia Schuster (cello); and Michael Coe (French horn), the last two chatted up at the entrance to the Royal Academy of Music and easily persuaded to be in a band without impeding their studies. We waited outside the Academy one day, and when somebody came in or out with a cello or French-horn case, we stopped him or her until we found our prospective new members. The group was completed by Ray (guitar and harmony vocals), Dave Preston (drums), and myself on vocals and guitar. Ray was adamant that we should be called Birth and nearly had his way, but I liked the word Karma; then Alex came up with Nirvana, after which there was no contest! We filled out a business-name registration form and sent it to an office in London EC1, from which it was returned—something to do with shares and limited companies; we had filled the wrong form, and the correct one was enclosed. We put it somewhere and forgot about it until another day.

We phoned the offices of George Martin, John Burgess, Denny Cordell, Chris Blackwell and Mickie Most a few days later, when we found out Most was in the same building in Oxford Street as Chris. They were the producers—talent finders at the forefront of the new pop revolution breaking out all over England, and believe me, things were moving fast. If you could not get your act together, you were gone even faster. We managed to make appointments with all of them for the following weeks and did some more work on our demos. George Martin never turned up for the appointment; we were asked to leave the tape—we never heard back. John Burgess was interested but needed a little more time; he was in the studio producing the Hollies. After hearing our demo and a live acoustic-guitar version of "Tiny Goddess" in the small music room at Oxford Street, Chris Blackwell signed us, on the spot, there and then, to a recording and publishing deal, with the seal of approval coming from American producer (just arrived in London) Jimmy Miller, who "air-mixed" with his athletic body, complex percussive patterns, accentuating the rhythm of the songs. We were introduced to Muff Winwood (A&R), Chris Peers (promotion) and Elsa (assistant to Chris), made a visit to "Neville the Accountant," where our signatures were exchanged for cash, and within the afternoon we were the first LP recording band to be signed to the original pink-labeled Island Records, the

Denmark's Best Sellers

This Week	Last Week	Weeks On Chart	
1	—	1	**Get Back** (Beatles/Apple-Parlophone) Dacapo Denmark
2	2	4	**Pigen og harbandet** (Bjorn & Okay/Polydor) D forlag, Denmark
3	6	3	**Goodbye** (Mary Hopkin/Apple) Dacapo Musikfor Denmark
4	1	5	**Casatschock** (Birthe Kjaer/CBS) Dacapo Musikf Denmark
5	3	4	**Sorry Suzanne** (Hollies/Parlophone)
6	5	5	**Don't Pass Me By** (Beatles/Apple-Parlophone) D Musikforlag, Denmark
7	—		**Rainbow Chaser** (Nirvana/Island Records)
8	4		**Ich sing ein Lied fur Dich** (Heintje/Philips)
9	9	2	**Boom Bang-A-Bang** (Lulu/Columbia) (Chappel N Sweden

Pentecost Hotel. Copyright © Blue Mountain Music 1968.

There underneath Blue Waves, the sunrise spreads blue rays
and Pentecost Hotel shakes all its cobwebs.
Explosion of the stars upon the sea in red
and all the guests that see the water fireworks.
And in the lobby, Magdalena is friendly
to all the people with a passport, of insanity and screen sirens are a dancing
to music in Pentecost Hotel - - —.
Strange viaduct of beams take me to all your dreams
And leave me there as master of the ocean
There underneath blue waves the sunshine spreads blue rays
and Pentecost Hotel shakes all its cobwebs.
Explosion of the stars upon the sea in Red, and all the guests
that see the Water Fireworks .....
And in the lobby Magdalena is friendly
and repeat.

Psychedelic Music

Written by Alex Spyropoulos and [illegible] Campbell-Lyons.

Published by Blue Mountain Music © 1968

PENTECOST HOTEL in C

THERE UNDER - - -

PIANO INTRO | C G/B | Am/A C/G | F/F C/E | Dm/D G/G | ½ G | (5 BARS)

VERSES | C G/B | Am/A C/G | F/F C/E | Dm/D /// | G /// | C /// |

| C G/B | Am/A C/G | F/F C/E | Dm/D /// | G /// | C/G ½ G | (12½ BARS)

CHORUS | C G/B | Am/A G/G |

| C G/B | Am/A G/G | (9½ BARS)

| C G/B | Am/A F | E Am | A♭ C | G /// | ½ G |

BACK, ALL THE WAY FROM VERSES + CHORUS (WITHOUT ½ G)

HARP INSTR/M | F C | D G | F C | D G | G /// DRM BREAK | (5 BARS)

CHORUS C G Am G
C G Am G
C G Am F | E Am | Ab C | G /// DRM BREAK | (9 BARS)

ENDING | C G | Am FG | over and over

RAINBOW CHASER IN C

INTRO | ROLL G/// | C E♭ | A♭ C | C E♭ | A♭ C | G /// | (6 BARS)

VERSE | C D | F G | C D | F G | Am E | C G | G HALF BAR

VERSE | " | " | " | " | " | | A♭ Fm | G/// | A♭ F | G/// | (12 BARS + 1/2)

CHORUS | C E♭ | A♭ C |
| C E♭ | A♭ C |
| C E♭ | A♭ C | G /// |

FROM THE TOP (7 BARS)

Verse

Travels on a Cloud, He's one of the good-time people now
I'm a face in the crowd all dressed up and laughing loud
I can't talk to him and I can't love him
Many miles to go, How many Bridges do you cross
Winter, rain and snow, over mountains high and low.
I can't talk to him, and I can't love him

Chorus. Vocal back-up oohs into Rainbow and Repeat.

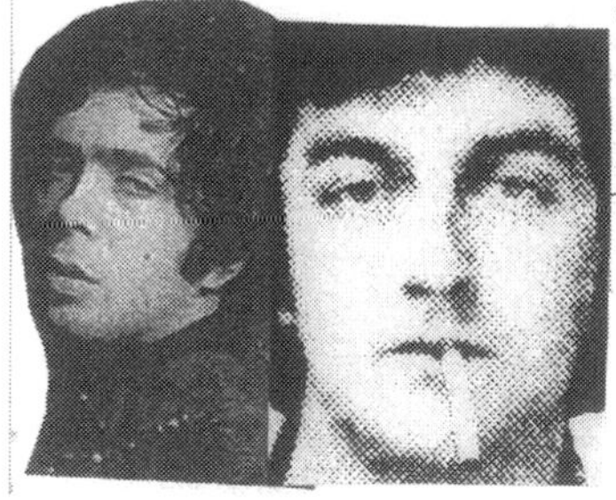

Written By
Alex Spyropoulos and Patrick Campbell-Lyons
Blue Mountain Music. ©1968

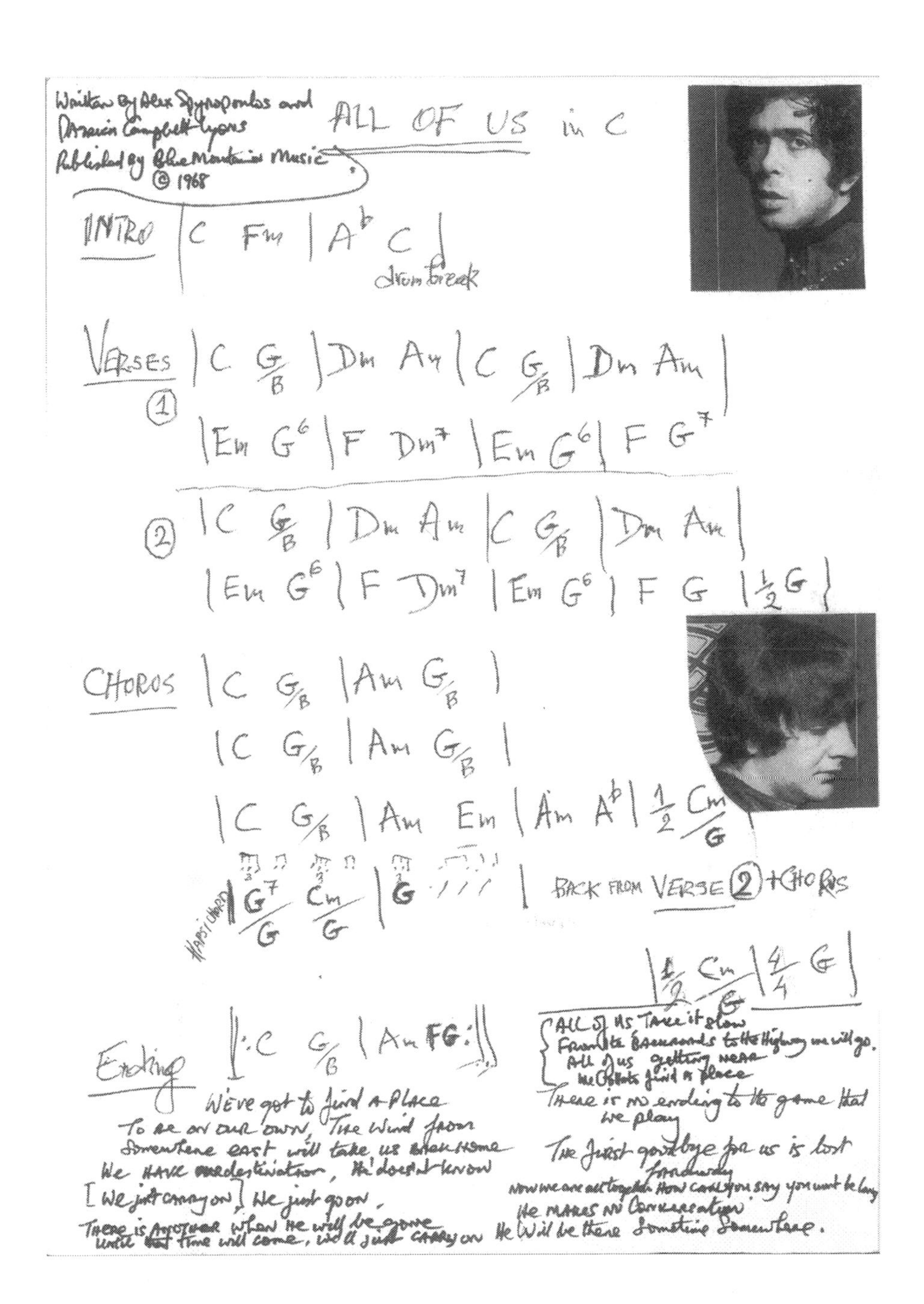

ALL OF US in C
© 1968
INTRO
drum break
VERSES
CHORUS
BACK FROM VERSE 2 + CHORUS
Ending
We've got to find a place
To be on our own, The wind from
somewhere east will take us
We just go on.
There is no ending to the game that
we play
He will be there sometime somewhere.

greatest independent ever. It has been the model to which every other independent recording company has cut its pattern, but it has never been equalled. We had become part of a new and vibrant family.

We kept our meeting with Mickie Most a few weeks later and used it to promote our songs to him. We played him the new songs that Alex and I had written a few days earlier, and which we were about to record for our own LP. He especially liked "Wings of Love" and said he would cut it with Herman's Hermits, who he was in the studio with over the next couple of evenings. A week later he left a message for us downstairs at the Island reception to come to De Lane Lea Studios in Holborn, and we could hear the finished recording and meet Peter Noone and the Hermits.

Mickie was a prolific song picker and producer, and so laid-back; everything he touched became gold in terms of record sales; positivity oozed from his every pore. He made you feel good by just being around him. We went to De Lane Lea, heard a great orchestral version of our song, met Pete and his boys from Manchester, and sitting in the biggest chair in the control room, smoking an even bigger cigar, was Allen

Klein, waiting to be upset by somebody—well, that was the impression he gave me. While we were there, a car came for him and Hermans Hermits to take them to the airport for a flight to New York, where they had a TV show to do before starting an American tour the next day.

A photo session was arranged for us with one of the top fashion/ music photographers of that time, Gered Mankowitz, and Nirvana was to be launched to the press and the public with a live show in early 1968 at the Saville Theatre in London's West End, sharing the bill with Traffic, Spooky Tooth and Jackie Edwards, a talented songwriter-singer who had come over from Jamaica with Chris Blackwell.

Our first stage performance received mixed reviews, and some of them were bizarre: "The music of Nirvana is like chamber music with a rock transfusion" . . . "classical pop with surrealistic overtones interwoven in the text" . . . "acid rock in a placid setting."

We had performed on a stage arranged like a drawing room (props from the theatre itself), and we were dressed in expensive silk Baluchi kaftans from Thea Porter Emporium, with Sylvia centre stage, the cello wedged between her legs, bow ready to strike. As the curtains opened to the first bars of "Tiny Goddess" on the cello, I could hear a gasp of amazement spread through the full house. The audience was not prepared for the spectacle or the sound. Five songs later, as the curtain closed and we faded on "I Believe in Magic," I felt as if I had been in a trance or at a séance.

It was a heady experience, but it taught me a lesson of survival in the risky business of selling yourself to an audience. Later that night at an Island celebration party in the Bag of Nails club, Jimmy Miller told me that the sound was pretty good even though the cello was badly amplified, but that our stage show and presentation "bordered on comedy." Willie Piggot-Brown, a racehorse trainer and farmer in Berkshire as well as a friend of Chris Blackwell's (Traffic were living in two cottages on Piggot-Brown's land, getting it together), said he enjoyed our show but that our stage act needed development, maybe even a rethink.

In any case, Alex and I decided the larger ensemble was not the route we wanted to take. With the total financial support and creative approval of Chris, towards the end of 1967 Alex and I disbanded the group and became a songwriting and recording duo who would tour and perform with different pickup orchestral musicians in the European capitals. In each city, the local promoter/agent would hire a group rhythm section of drums, bass, guitar and keyboards, and bring in strings, brass and percussion from the city orchestras. We would take with us the scores and the arrangements that had been written up by the brilliant Syd Dale for our studio recordings, have a full rehearsal in the late afternoon and do the show that night . . . and it worked for us.

"Rainbow Chaser" had entered the charts in England, France, Germany and Scandinavia. Copenhagen was our first stop.

Indulgent Recommendation for the iPod Generation

Traffic, live concert at Fillmore East, New York, Nov. 18, 1970 (YouTube)

Françoise Hardy, «Je Ne Sais Pas Ce Que Veux» ("Tiny Goddess") (You Tube)

Syd Dale, *Retro: Original Tracks From the Amphonic Archives* (1960s)

THE FLYING MUSHROOM
Guy Stevens, 1967-68

He jumped into the flames and danced the dance of the "Flying Mushroom"

Harlequin, shaman, disc doctor, illuminated by the light of the purple moon. He flew through the canyons of London Town, always in the moment, in rhythm with its heartbeat, its sounds reverberating around him.

The first time I saw Guy Stevens was at the "Middle Earth" nights, a regular "happening" near Oxford Street in late 1967. Then I saw him everywhere—the marquee in Wardour Street, the Ship pub, La Chaise (a private dive for the drinking fraternity of that square mile of Soho), the Roundhouse on a Sunday, Portobello Road on a Saturday. He was the original UFO, the Fourteen Hour (Technicolour) Dream, Granny Takes a Trip, all in the same person at the same time.

Then one day in that same year he was facing me on the stairway at the Island Records office in Oxford Street. Before I could say, "What's happening!" he was giving me the history of the graphics team Hapsash and the Coloured Coat, and instructing me on the exceptional talents of the group Art, who were about to become Spooky Tooth. (He was the producer and mentor of both these projects.) Guy lit up a healthy-looking joint and put it in my hand, telling me to be extra careful, because he and I were the people our parents warned us against. He left me with the spliff with "Have a blast, man!" Then he was gone, levitated out of the building, an amalgam of mushroom cloud, Afro hairstyle, sheepskin waistcoat, long rainbow scarf, cherry red flares over green handmade Cuban heel boots . . . He was a one-off, a special kind of man.

That's how it was to be over the next months when I went to the Island office. Guy was usually there in all his glory—talent scout, art director, writer, Sue label specialist, Chuck Berry Fan Club organiser, producer, image maker, and ideas/publicity man. He was brainstorming and multi-tasking 35 years before the words became cliché. On top of all that, Guy was a DJ at the Scene Club, where he had built up a loyal following—mostly musicians, because he played imports that were difficult to find; you needed American contacts. I would say that Guy Stevens, and Alexis Korner a few years earlier, were the two most important and innovative people in sourcing and introducing this material for the London rock and roll bands of the '60s.

Guy had an originality that I never saw again, anywhere. He had a thing about numbers, and we had something in common there; we were both born on the 13th day of the month in the same year, 1943—he in April, I in July, and since he was three months older than me, that was "good for the vibes, man!" If the vibes were not right, Guy did not stick around. Three and 13 were two of his good-vibe numbers, so I was an "Oobladee," and if you did not have the good-vibe numbers, for him you were an "Oobladaa" and he blanked you out.

We had another thing in common: We liked the bluebeat and ska singles out of Jamaica. I invited him one Saturday lunchtime to a place on Melbourne Avenue in West Ealing called the Black Bomber Café, where I used to hang out during my Ealing days. The Mod guys who ran the place were real pillheads, and the Rockola jukebox, which was on continual rotation, had only bluebeat, except on rare occasions introducing a couple of new singles that were beginning to get popular. Otherwise it was Prince Buster, Laurel Aitken, Derrick Morgan, Owen Gray, and the Skatellites. My two favourite singles were "Housewives' Choice" by Derrick and Patsy, and "Oh Carolina" by the Folks Brothers.

Little did I know that five years later I would be signing a recording contract with Chris Blackwell, the man responsible for bringing that music to England. Guy appreciated my interest in blue beat, and we spent all day blagging over coffees and mandies, continuously moving to the groove. Later that night we found ourselves in a small, dingy basement near Brewer Street Market in Soho called the Limbo Club, a regular haunt for Mods and pillheads where you only heard bluebeat and ska. About 4 in the morning, the place was raided by a team of detectives and Special Police with dogs. We were all marched outside to an alley, where we were handcuffed, searched, led away to the waiting wagons and transported over to West End Central Police Station. (On the way, Guy told me, "Have no worries, man. I have a good brief!") I don't remember too much more about it, other than most of us being released without charge about 7 in the morning and ending up on Regent Street cold, hungry and with a massive comedown. Later that night, I went to see the Soft Machine at the Roundhouse, but Guy was not there; someone told me he had been busted.

The music that Alex and I were making as Nirvana was far too ethereal for Guy's taste, so on that front we had very little in common. He spent his Island creative time with Spooky Tooth, Traffic and later Mottle the Hoople. Every so often I saw him jumping into the flames at some club or "happening" in London, but as our music was beginning to take off in Europe and the words "itinerary" and "travel arrangement" became an important part of our work, I lost sight of him for some time. We were now much in demand in Germany, Scandinavia, France and Holland, and "Rainbow Chaser," our single, was becoming a hit record; it had to be promoted.

From the beginning, Guy had taken to calling me "Christy the Gypsy" for some reason known only to him, and I christened him "the Flying Mushroom." You see, with Guy it was all about speed, action, fantasy, kicks, good dialogue, and massive contradiction on comedown time.

Denny Cordell, who was across the street from Island, had around this time signed a band called Procol Harum to his company; Guy knew them and was friendly with Keith Reid, the lyricist. Guy was doing a number on me about them being a "great fucking signing." I asked him how he could like them, as they were not his kind of bag; in fact, they were ploughing a similar furrow as ourselves but without the orchestral arrangements. He angrily responded, "Don't ever fucking question my musical taste, man." We shut up shop for the rest of the night.

About a year later we were back around the London scene again to record a new album. On a visit to Island Records for a meeting, I enquired of Guy from Elsa, Chris Blackwell's P.A., only to learn that he was taking an extended holiday for possession courtesy of HMP. When he had served his time he went on the missing list; it was four years later that I saw Guy again, on the night that Chuck Berry played the Speakeasy Club. Guy was in his element with so many faces around. He had a shirt with coloured lights on, which he controlled from a switch in his trouser pocket. He was flying, but everybody else was on the same flight. When Berry hit the opening chords of "Carol," the place went mental—the Flying Mushroom was the Satellite Jockey.

Over the following years I kept contact with Dave Betteridge, who moved from Island to CBS Records; he sent me an invite to the launch party of the Clash LP *London Calling*. It took place in the ballroom of the Park Lane Hotel. The whole atmosphere felt really uncomfortable and corporate—that is, until Guy (who had produced the album) made his flying entrance. He stormed through the room in a white silk suit, sequined scarf and waistcoat, and purple Cubans. He was "Right on!" in your face and unfortunately upstaging the band, who were just going through the motions of the event. It was obvious that he did not know where he was or what was happening, nor did he care. His departure was swiftly and discreetly organised when his display of manic behaviour began to embarrass the suits who had organised the launch party. For Guy it mattered nothing, because he saw them all as "Oobladaas" . . . and he was right.

The final time I saw Guy was out of the blue—or maybe that should be out of the morning mist—two years later, in 1980. We were recording at Virtual Earth Studios right by Swiss Cottage in NW3. Alex and I had written a musical called *Bloood* and were under pressure, due to a limited budget, to finish the complete cast recordings in a week. We were paying the bills, so the deadline had to be met. I needed to get some fresh air, as we had been working through the night, so at about 8 o'clock in the morning I took a walk. I found myself in a small public play area. I sat there for a while in peaceful meditation. As I left to go back to the studio, I saw in a corner just inside the gate three dishevelled-looking men in a sorry state of inebriation and was shocked to recognise Guy as one of them. "Guy," I said, approaching right next to them. The only response was incoherent mumbling. Guy was in a very dark place; nobody could reach him. It was difficult to handle. I have never spoken about it until now, not even to Alex when I returned to the studio.

Guy went to meet his Reverend Creator in August of the following year, 1981. I have thought of him often. When I do, considering the fallibility of rock and roll memory, I'm amazed by the energy of his presence—the detail in those recollections, even to the point of being able to read the title on whichever book he is holding. He craved knowledge, stimulated by the subtlety of the written word. I never saw him without a book; he is the only person I know who read *Mein Kampf*, Adolf Hitler's Nazi Bible, cover to cover. Guy had a permanent copy on his desk in the Island Records office . . . don't ask me why! Guy could take you to the instant gratification of youth; he could also touch your soul. I don't miss him, because he is always around in my galaxy. But I miss that kind of brilliant company, impossible to find today . . . or tomorrow.

YOU CAN ALL JOIN IN
Island and the First Sampler, 1969

It was between 8 and 9 o'clock in the capital, sometime in early October 1969; I remember the silver blue of the sunlight on the unwelcome frost. Hyde Park London was beautiful but cold, one of those prickly mornings that made your eyes water and your nose run. There were a lot of wooly hats, scarves, army coats around the place; Traffic's Jim Capaldi was the only one wearing shades.

Penny Hansen, a real gem of a lady from Island, turned up with flasks of tea and coffee; sandwiches appeared as if by miracle from a suitcase that had seen better days. An array of combustibles were doing the rounds, prepared by the experts amongst the gathering, to be shared by all the cast.

Aubrey Powell, the photographer, part of the Hipgnosis design team, arrived on the scene with a grand stepladder, proceeded to climb to its summit, perched himself there like a vulture strapped with camera equipment, and drew us into the shuttered frame, imploring the group Free to come up front because of their lack of height.

"The Incredible Occasion," "A Crazy Scenario," a brainwave of Chris Blackwell, our mentor, was instigated a week earlier, when he said, "Just try to be there. You can all join in." It was to be a photo session for the sleeve of Island's compilation album *You Can All Join In* (the title came from a song by Dave Mason of Traffic), so we were there, to a man . . . even to a woman, the wonderful Sandy Denny, Fairport Convention's vocalist, the only female artist in the picture. Traffic and their roadie arrived from the country in a mud-splattered jeep; others were in London, up all night or just rolled out of someone's bed.

Alex and I had been to the Speakeasy Club, an all-nighter in Margaret Street W1. It must have been a Friday, because everybody turned up later at Island Records to collect our weekly retainers—except for Nick Drake, who never left his apartment; he had Joy Boyd collect it for him. We were getting 30 pounds a week each; my rent was only eight pounds. We lived like kings! Spooky Tooth got the same as us; I think Traffic were on a little more. Each band had an allowance for stagewear, which we spent at the Thea Porter Emporium—a shrine of creativity in Soho where she designed handmade kaftans and waistcoats using the Baluchi style of sewing tiny mirrors on the silk cloth, typical of parts of India and Pakistan. We dressed in our new stage gear for the first time when we appeared with Salvador Dali on a Paris television show. We were promoting the release of our single, "Pentecost Hotel," in France/Belgium. Free had bought their army coats that morning, especially for the occasion, and Andy Fraser, their bassist, told me that they cost three pounds from a stall in Notting Hill Market.

The shot that was used for the sleeve of the album was chopped, not cropped, and a small group of the band members on the left side, about ten, were lost to posterity. Chris had planned it to be a gatefold, but the production costs restricted that idea. Nobody was really bothered about it; the attitude was that we were one big family, and it had been a great day out for everyone who made it there. I found my own place in the photograph, for no other reason than to be surrounded by bodies for warmth from the cold morning. Ian A. Anderson, the Manfred Mann look-alike in the centre of the group, had just been signed to the label; his solo album *Stereo Death Breakdown* was about to be released. When Ian Anderson of Jethro Tull realised that some confusion might prevail, he insisted that it be sorted at the last hour; Island replaced the Ian A. track with the Spencer Davis Group's "Somebody Help Me," a song written by Jackie Edwards, one of my favourite people in that original Island family, whom Chris had encouraged to come to England from Jamaica.

Many of the artists on the album went on to achieve success, fame and respect in the music world; it was a Number 1 on the charts. The sales of the artists on *You Can All Join In* were boosted to another level, which was the real purpose behind the brilliant concept. It was the first ever "sampler," copied by every other company in the following years. Chris Blackwell, Dave

Betteridge and Guy Stevens were innovators who were "concepting" and creating in the same way that the bands were. They got off on music with a passion, and with the business end of things Chris and David knew how to make a deal, but always with respect for the other side. Guy Stevens was not in the least interested in business.

Barry Winton, a well-known record collector and music writer, introduced himself to me in the late '80s as a fan of Nirvana. During an interview about my production work on Vertigo Records, we started to discuss prized and precious records in our collections. He invited me to his apartment in London to impress me with his 5,000-plus albums. He told me that the first LP he ever owned was *You Can All Join In*, bought for him by his mum as a 10th birthday present. He had asked for it after hearing "Rainbow Chaser" by Nirvana on the radio. My reaction was a mixture of surprise and humour; I told him tongue in cheek that I hoped he was not holding me responsible for his obsession with vinyl.

I find it difficult to understand why Barry and others in that collecting world would buy three, maybe four copies of the same LP and put them away in protective covers, never to be played or shared! On the other hand, maybe someday he will donate or "trust" his collection to a music museum or university library . . . or make a killing on eBay . . . more likely!

Our Nirvana track "Rainbow Chaser," featured on "You Can All Join In," has become a pop psychedelic classic; it has appeared on many compilations worldwide, including *Back on the Road* (Stylus Records), *The Psychedelic Years Revisited* (Sequel Records), and *Traveling on a Cloud,* the Nirvana UK best-of collection on Island, Polygram and Universal Records; it was a Number 1 single in Scandinavia and entered the charts in England, France, Germany and Australia. Most important for us, it was also released in the USA on Volume 9 of Rhino Records' *The British Invasion* series. This LP was a vital piece of evidence in our litigation process with the Seattle group Nirvana on Geffen Records in the early '90s.

It was important for our legal people to show that we had an American profile, that our music was available in their record stores. We based ourselves for three weeks in L.A. as part of the legal process that was going to take place. I well remember the day in 1992 that Alex and I decided to wander into Tower Records on Sunset Boulevard on the off chance that we would find something of ours for sale there. We typed the title "Rainbow Chaser" into a touch-screen computer; it sent us to a section of the store titled "Golden Oldies," where we found one copy of *The British Invasion Vol. 9*. We made the purchase, got a dated receipt, took a cab from Sunset Boulevard to Century City and smiled our way up to our lawyer's office on the 28th floor . . . A result:

On the way down, we shared the elevator with Ali MacGraw, the actress who played the female lead in the Oscar Award-winning movie *Love Story*, one of the most popular tearjerkers ever. She heard us talking, turned around and said, "Where do you come from in Ireland? I always love to hear that accent." She told us that her father was Irish-American, and that she went regularly to visit and party there with friends. I remember thinking, this is the ex-wife of the actor Steve McQueen; also the wife of Robert Evans, the Hollywood producer, two of the most difficult men in the movie business. She is in her early '50s and radiantly attractive. What would happen if I tried to chat her up? Then the doors opened and as they did, I said, “That’s a lovely perfume you’re wearing. What is it?” and she said “It’s Yoga,” and she was gone with a smile and a wave.

It was a good day in L.A.

JIMI HENDRIX AND THE PSYCHEDELIC CELLO OF LOVE
1966-68

Like a comet crashing into Earth from outer space, Jimi Hendrix hit London town on September 23, 1966, and the whirlwind that followed blew everyone away. Clapton, Townshend and Page, the guitar gods of the age, went into a short secret retirement, took another look at their chord structures and tried to absorb the shock of the lesson they had been given by the new master. They had jammed with him or he had jammed with them, and the force of nature that was Jimi and his Fender Stratocaster was not an experience they wished to encounter again; it was better to stand back and let the tornado spin itself forward and on, which is what they did . . . you can't lasso a tornado! I was witness to one of those legendary jams at the Speakeasy Club in Margaret Street, London, but it was not the first time I saw Jimi.

A few days before, Hendrix's bassist Noel Redding—whom Alex and I knew well, as he had played on a number of demos for us—brought Jimi into La Gioconda Café in Denmark Street for a cuppa. Noel had a bit of a soft spot for Alex's girlfriend at that time, Eva, who was from Paris, and if we were there with her when Noel came in, always with his two guitar cases, he would come over and join us and have a good flirt with Eva, who like all beautiful French women was an expert at playing that game.

Noel, with his round wire-framed specs and his bird's nest of an Afro, enjoyed a good laugh if things were going well, but he could be moody. He was always looking for a place to stay the night and kip on the floor. He had come up by train from the South Coast somewhere and would remain in London for as many days as he had sessions, playing guitar and bass on songwriters' and publisher demos or on fledgling masters. He would also audition for new bands who were looking for musicians through the *Melody Maker*, the musicians' bible, and did gigs with up-and-coming singers who were making some impact, like Gene Latter ("Just a Little Piece of Leather"); Alex Harvey, who had just come down from Scotland; Jack Hammer from somewhere out there; and John Christian Dee. Like the rest of us, they all used the Gioconda as their office. They would recruit a pickup band in a matter of hours and do the gig that night . . . if they could find a van and a roadie.

Mitch Mitchell, on the other hand, I had not seen for about two years. He was not into songwriting, so Denmark Street had not become a focal point in his search for the big time as a drummer, but I'm sure he was working on a regular basis, because Mitch was a very regular and basic kind of person who never left home without a pair of drumsticks. My lasting memory of Mitch would always be from the earlier Ealing days and the sound of his playing drums coming from Jim Marshall's Music Shop and Drum Emporium, the waves of his percusiveness rolling into Hanwell and along the Uxbridge Road. If he was in the local café during his break from the shop, where he was the drums salesman, he would be playing on the table, the cups and the plates; if you met him on the 207 bus, he was tapping out his rhythms on the rail of the seat in front of him. He talked endlessly and passionately the drummers' language about paradiddles (complicated rhythm patterns on the snare drum), about cymbals (with or without rivets), about what was best, Ludwig or Premier. If he wasn't playing a gig at the weekend, he was practising, and during the week in the shop, he was fulfilling his role in getting other drummers of the future to put down a hire-purchase deposit on a new kit by showing them how it was done for real.

When I saw Noel with Jimi Hendrix that first time at the Gio, he made no mention of Mitch. I think they were still trying out drummers; all he said was, "This is Jimi from New York; we're going to have a band together," and that was it. Noel was a very laid-back person and was not easily impressed, but there was something about him that day that was different, and within a few months, that something was the Experience.

When they came into the Gio, neither the men nor the women could take their eyes off Jimi. The chicks were melting in the patchouli perfume of his presence—this child of the universe, this man from the skies, this exotic creature with smouldering charm, this Cherokee gypsy with rainbow scarf and candy-coloured shirt, this travellin' man who was blown away by London black cabs, red double-decker buses, Big Ben and the Houses of Parliament, fish and chips, and going in the pub. Hendrix was an acid dandy, a black psychedelic hippie with shy eyes and lips burnt from too much sweet kissing. (A girl I knew who had a scene with Jimi for a short while told me, "With Jimi you just succumb without reservations." "What a beautiful way to describe being fucked," I said to her. "Yes, and it was beautiful," she told me.

Jimi was all this and more. Imagine then what it was like when this king of Venus took his Strat in his long, elegant hands, strapped it over his shoulder, and with electrified fingers dripping in sustain and reverb, sliding and riding the chords of "Purple Haze," "Hey Joe" or "Little Wing" . . . It was the birth of the new psychedelic blues.

"Impossible" is not a word Jimi recognized when it came to making music. For him, the extraordinary was mundane. When he did a show, he gave you the visual experience as well as the emotional, movement and constant change, "Now you see it, now you don't." In just over two years, Jimi Hendrix and the Experience made three of the greatest albums ever recorded in the rock-pop music pantheon . . . *Are you Experienced* (1967), Axis: *Bold as Love* (January 1968) and *Electric Ladyland* (October 1968). The contribution of creative energy and passion that Noel and Mitch put into recording and touring the world should never be underestimated. Jimi and the Experience were the real deal, and though the group's life span was short, the sound they made together, and the essence of spirit that was Jimi, combined to make a music that meant so much to so many then and now, and will continue to do so in the future.

The next time I saw Jimi I met him, and Sylvia Schuster with her cello was the conduit. Sylvia knew nothing whatsoever of the pop-rock world; she was from a strict and straight classical-music background. A good Jewish girl, married, with a child on the way . . . how she ever agreed to follow Alex and me on the Nirvana trip remains a mystery to me. I suspected that with such musical talent and virtuosity as a cellist, she was curious as to what other musicians might be doing in their world. Making pop music was to her an alien form, yet she threw herself with abandon into the new experience and told me after a week of rehearsal that she was beginning to enjoy the freedom it gave her to experiment and improvise arrangements, unheard of in the classical sacredness of the Academy where she studied.

In fact, underneath the serious musician exterior, there was a cheeky, bubbly Sylvia that brought an infectious radiance, colour and texture to our sound. We knew, however, that the cello was her business, her livelihood, and that the classical world would be her stage in the not-too-distant future. It was her love, and She went on to become principal cellist with many of the well-known English orchestras.

It was magical to watch her play once she realised after a few days with us that it was fucking liberating for her not to have the score in front of her on the music stand; it was beautiful to hear her solo. On the other hand, if Michael Coe, the French horn player, who was just as brilliant on his instrument, had not come along for the ride, I don't think Sylvia would have come on her own with the two hippies standing outside on the Academy steps.

We were contracted to appear on a BBC TV show to perform "Pentecost Hotel," our newest song, which was getting massive airplay, especially on John Peel's programme. The show was being produced at the BBC West Hampstead Studio, and it was to be a challenging experience for us. We would have to record the complete song all over again in six hours, to master quality for broadcast a few days later. I did a guide vocal for everybody in their headphones, and when the backing track was acceptable (quality control was important always with the "Beeb" in those days), the take that the in-house engineers, not us, decided on was overdubbed with a new vocal and harmony. In other words, it would be a complete new recording as close as possible to the original.

The BBC in-house engineers and producers that were around in those days were technically brilliant but very reluctant to take risks, which we definitely were, so it was somewhat compromising, but we were well aware that we had to get it right on the day; we had worked on the original recording over the period of a week. We were having some problems with the microphone placement and pickup on the cello, and Sylvia was being very patient and good-humoured about the situation, which required her to play her part over and over for the engineer. The electric cello in a rock-band scenario was a new experience for studio people . . . in fact I believe we were the first to use one in the pop-group context. It's a Beautiful Day, a band from the West Coast of America that Alex liked, featured an electric violin, and Love, an L.A. band featuring songwriters Arthur Lee and Bryan MacLean, was about to release one of my all-time favourite albums, the stunning *Forever Changes*, with amazing cello and viola arrangements by Bruce Botnik and David Angel.

It was while we were between takes that the Jimi Hendrix Experience appeared in the studio—first Noel, then Mitch, and then the Maestro himself; they were on the show to promote "Hey Joe." As they walked across the room in a single file, Jimi stopped to hear Sylvia's playing, stood for a minute or two, came back towards the centre and sat crosslegged on the floor opposite us, captivated by the sound she was making. He stayed there for the next 10 minutes, listening to us do takes of "Pentecost Hotel." At one point, he moved his chair to be in a better position to see how she was playing; he was like a kid looking at a new guitar in a shop window.

When Sylvia played, she was like Jimi—stroking and caressing, plucking and attacking those four strings—and he sat there in gentle rapture. At one point we stopped, and Sylvia called me over from the microphone and asked quietly, "Why is that man staring at me like that? Who is he?" I said, "That's Jimi Hendrix!" His name meant nothing to her, but that was no fault of hers; she was a complete stranger in our world of pop and rock. When he was leaving, as we had finished another take, he came over and said, "Good luck with the song, guys." Then he turned towards Sylvia: "Excuse me ma'am, I just want to say I love what you do." She turned deep red, but with a twinkle in her eye, she replied, "You are very kind. Thank you." His charm was effortless; if you could bottle it like perfume, it would have made you a fortune.

When we had packed up our gear and were about to leave the building, we could hear Jimi, Mitch and Noel laying down the track for "Hey Joe." It was fucking heavy, man. Noel's driving bass line was tearing through the soundproof walls; the engineers must have been shitting themselves—there was no way that sound could be compressed or limited.

About a month later, I encountered Jimi again, this time in the Bag of Nails Pub, where I was meeting Viv Prince, the drummer of the Pretty Things. Jimi was sitting at the bar with Chas Chandler, who had been the bass player with the Animals but was now managing the Experience. Jimi remembered me but got the name of our group wrong; he thought we were called Nevada. He told me that he had never seen a cello before that day; he liked the sound of our band, because it was original. "You know, man, playing with that instrument is like making love, those deep tones and colours . . . that cello between her legs. Man, it made me happy . . . Have a drink." I think they were both a bit out of their heads, but it was a very true moment that will always travel with me, as the immortal Jimi Hendrix still travels on.

The last song that Jimi wrote was "The Story of Life": "The story of life is quicker than the wink of an eye/The story of love is hello and goodbye until we meet again." He was found dead in a flat in Holland Park, London, the next day, September 18, 1970.

Indulgent Recommendation for the iPod Generation

If you are reading this book, I am sure you already know the main albums of Jimi Hendrix and the Experience. So I would recommend something a little more obscure:

***Jimi Plays Monterey/Shake! Otis Redding* (Criterion DVD, recorded 1967)**

Bo Diddley, *Bo Diddley Is a Gunslinger* (Chess, 1963)

Otis Redding, *Pain in My Heart* (Atco, 1964)

Don Covay, "Mercy, Mercy" (1964; Jimi played guitar)

GOLDEN EARS
Mickie Most

Some people can smell gold, others can feel where it is hiding, but Mickie Most could hear gold, and when he did, he knew how to turn tiny flecks into huge nuggets; that is why I called him "Golden Ears." His office was an open space on the floor above Island Records at 155-157 Oxford Street, London W1, and it had four desks—one for Mickie; one for his brother Dave Most, who was the publisher and promoter; and two for Peter Grant, who was big.

As the Most Brothers, Mickie and Alex Wharton

had come from South Africa to try to make it on the new exploding British pop scene, but they were clever enough to recognise their limitations as a rock and roll act competing with the local favourites Cliff Richard, Marty Wilde, Tommy Steele, Billy Fury and Adam Faith at the legendary 2 I's Café at 59 Old Compton Street where it was all taking off. They decided their real talent was in finding and producing new groups and singers, and over the next decade, their success was remarkable.

The Mosts were both handsome young men with star-quality personas; they opened important doors easily with their charisma and charm. They had a mutual respect, but Mickie was the boss. Peter Grant had been a professional wrestler turned bouncer who worked at the 2 I's Café; Mickie brought him into the treble winning formula as the management. In the '60s, they ruled supreme as a production company; there was no one to touch them as far as getting hit records, mostly (pun unavoidable) Number 1's on both sides of the Atlantic. The method was simple: Mickie found the song and the act and produced them in the studio; Dave published and promoted the song and the record when it was released; and Peter set up the tours.

Mickie had time for songwriters. We were his lifeblood, after all, and the song was everything in those days—not like now, when a tune or a melody is a hindrance to the rhythm, and a good lyric is deemed too clever for the short attention span of the multitasking, brainwashed consumer kid. Mickie listened to thousands of songs; they came by post, by messenger bike or, if the songwriters knew Mickie or had some track record with him, they would bring their demos in for a playing session. For us, it was a flight of stairs to the next floor, but we never abused the facility of his listening time, because we knew you had to have a good enough song, even in its simplest demo form, even to think about going up there. His desk and the floor space around it were always covered—in an orderly fashion, I must clarify—with tapes and vinyl white-label demos. Every songwriter was hoping Mickie would produce a song with one of his groups; we were successful when he cut "Wings of Love," a song we had written for our first LP, *The Story of Simon Simopath*, with Herman's Hermits from Manchester, who were scoring big in America—their "Something Good" was Number 1 there.

Mickie's warm personality always put one at ease when playing him weeks of work in a few nervous minutes. He had the ability to make me feel I could go away and improve my songwriting and my approach to recording, because his analysis of our songs was always constructive. He knew he had the gift to spot the magic in a song, and it was never difficult for him to tell you that your demo "just does not make it, this time!" He knew in the first 30 seconds if a song had it or not, and I honestly believe that he listened to everything that came into his office.

It was on Mickie's advice that "Rainbow Chaser," our British chart hit, still radio-played today, was swapped over from its "B"-side status ("Girl in the Park" was the official "A" side) to become our best-selling song worldwide. Pentecost Hotel entered the charts in Australia and Germany, and it was a "turntable hit" in England thanks to the radio play John Peel, Dave Cash, Mike Lennox and John Walker gave it on the BBC. We had been to see Mickie with some songs and asked him if he had time to listen to our new single, which he did . . . All he said was, "Go down and tell Chris that 'Rainbow Chaser' should be the 'A' side." We said something like,

"I think the labels have been printed already," and his reply was "Change them." He was right.

On another occasion we played Mickie a song we really believed in called "All of Us," which we had recorded for our second album. We thought it would make a great cover for Terry Reid, whom Mickie was about to produce. He did not see it, telling us it would be a good song for a movie, "But I'm not in the movie business." A few months later, we were in the Island Records music room, playing some demos of ours to Tony Visconti, who was going to do a string arrangement for us on the album. We did not know it at the time, but a meeting was taking place in Chris Blackwell's office with Stevie Winwood and Spencer Davis (who had written and recorded the title song for a film called *Here We Go Round the Mulberry Bush*) and some people from 20th Century-Fox Film Company. The meeting was about the two writing and recording a song for the studio's new production, *The Touchables.* Stevie turned it down on the basis that they were too busy touring and recording a new album, and as Chris was escorting the production people to the hall, one of them heard us in the music room playing *"All of Us" and said, "That would be a perfect song for The Touchables*. What is it?" We were introduced, they listened to it a few times, and that afternoon Chris signed the deal for us and we re-recorded it in Pye Studios at Marble Arch a week later as the title song of the film. The four actresses—Judy Huxtable, Marilyn Rickard, Esther Anderson and Kathy Simmonds—and the male lead, David Anthony, sang the vocals with us. Mickie Most was right again.

The film was released the following year and the soundtrack was eclectic to say the least, with songs by the Beatles, Otis Redding, Wynder K. Frog and Nirvana.

We had been in the right place at the right time—half the battle, my dad used to say. The film has become a cult classic on the psychedelia-mod "B"-movie circuit and is regularly featured at festivals such as "Mods and Rockers" at the Egyptian Theatre in Hollywood, California. The screenplay was by Ian La Frenais, and the director was Robert Freeman. Jimmy Miller and Chris Blackwell produced the soundtrack with Ken Thorne.

For us at that time, it was a big deal: Just over a year earlier we were sitting in La Gioconda trying to visualise our concept of Nirvana, and now here we were with screen credits on a film for 20th Century-Fox.

That was the beauty of the music business then—the unpredictability, the possibility of striking gold, digging deep to find the vein. And for a while there between 1964 and 1970, Mickie Most found a wide seam.

The other amazing aspect to Mickie's productions was his focus, his knowing exactly what he wanted to hear on the finished master recording, and how he went about getting it. Not for him a day to get the drum sound, or constant overdubbing and re-recording of different parts, or doing "drop-ins" where mistakes or glitches occurred—that was all "fannying about" as far as he was concerned. He did a track in a day, finished and out, and it was a 12-hour day, with the "B" side included. He put the backing tracks down in the morning, the vocals, lead and harmony in the afternoon, he mixed in the evening, and he was at home with his missus before midnight. The take went to the cutting plant the next morning, and the record was in the shops within a week. He worked the same way when he produced a 12-track L.P.

Every time Mickie Most struck gold—and it had to be an American *Billboard* Number 1 single or album by his standards—it was there for all to see on the walls of the office. He liked his gold records, did Mickie, and the place was a gallery of them, presented by the chart industries in America, England and Japan to him as the producer of millions of units sold. People bought 45 rpm singles in those days as often as they bought a packet of cigarettes; today you can get to Number 1 by selling 50,000—what a joke! Then it was more in the region of 250,000, or quite often more, and the competition was ferocious; everyone wanted some of the action, as the potential was huge.

Mickie's office was always a hub of activity, with "names and faces" sitting around at the desks, on the carpet and on the big cushions that were scattered everywhere. I recall we went up there late one afternoon. We had met on the stairs earlier in the day, and he said to our request to play him something, "Come up and see me later." Jeff Beck, he of "Hi Ho Silver Lining," produced by Mickie, opened the door. "Come on in, lads. Mickie is on the phone." Donovan was sitting in the corner strumming a guitar; he introduced us to his dad, who was his unofficial manager at the time, and to Gypsy Dave, his bongo man. Terry Reid was talking to Peter Grant at his desk, and Ashley Kozak, a well-known jazz bassist from the late-'50s London scene, was asleep or possibly meditating in Dave Most's swivel chair; Ashley had just come back from India after spending a year there, and was about to become Donovan's full-time manager.

I thought, "Fuck me, we are going to have to play our song demos to Mickie when he gets off the phone, and this starry amalgam of leather and beads will be hearing our stuff" . . . and that's how it was, but it was cool. You could play songs to him on the guitar as Donovan did, or song demos as we did, and Jeff Beck was working on a rough mix of something. There were no prima donna antics; everybody was equal, and the atmosphere was more of a listening jam session than anything else.

To keep the record straight, Mickie did have a few projects that, as the Americans say, tanked, none more so than the first LP of Terry Reid, whom he also managed until they had a falling-out in 1969. But with so many hits to his name, the odd miss here and there was an inevitability.

Like a handful of others, Mickie "Golden Ears" Most created a glittering musical path into the future from a difficult and uncertain musical past, and that's why the songs continue to live 40 years later.

Indulgent Recommendation for the iPod Generation

Jeff Beck, "Hi Ho Silver Lining"

The Animals, "House of the Rising Sun"

Lulu, "To Sir with Love"

Herman's Hermits, No Milk Today" and "Something Good"

. . . all million-sellers for "Golden Ears"

INTO MOROCCO
Paul Bowles, Jimmy Miller, the Pan Pipes of Jajouka, Cheb Khaled, 1969

When I was 14, I met the amazing Mr. Cleary. He was my geography lay teacher at Catholic Christian Brothers Secondary School in the Republic of Ireland; he also taught me history. The seeds of geographical wanderlust that he planted in me still flourish today.

Just like Hannibal at the head of his Carthaginian soldiers, Mr. Cleary stood proudly and defiantly at the front of his class, mesmerizing us with his knowledge. A guru, a guide, he could take us wherever he desired . . . spinning the globe of the world! Suddenly! with his pointer stick he would give it a positive yet gentle prod, and wherever the point landed when the spinning stopped, that's where we went with him for that lesson. He was a fountain of facts, always able to make the journey exciting and memorable, yet he had never travelled anywhere himself. His son who was in my year told me that his father, about 55 at that time, left our town only once, and that was to attend his daughter's wedding in Cork City, 60 miles away.

Towards the end of his geography lesson, Mr. Cleary would always give one of us the chance to go somewhere of our own choice. Like the other boys in the class, I was always ready . . . "Padraig"—I heard my name! (We spoke Irish and English for every subject, except Irish of course, in that school.) "The river Zambesi, sir" was my instant reply. Down the Zambesi, the fourth-longest river in Africa, I took the class and Mr. "Hannibal" Cleary by canoe, over rapids and falls, past crocodiles and rhinoceros, over Victoria Falls, the largest in the world, and without capsizing, I triumphantly paddled into the waves of the Indian Ocean after an adventure of 1,600 miles.

After that, I felt I could go anywhere—everything was possible. In the early '60s, around the time of the Second Thoughts, I realised that music was a passport to travel the world, meet unusual and sometimes crazy people, in unlikely situations and unexpected places, and have adventures. This realisation motivated me to take every chance to travel that came my way, either with Nirvana or independently, the latter appealing much more to my nomadic, gypsy ways.

Wherever I went, I had the music in me, and sometimes I found it in someone else, but those special ones don't stay around too long. The idea of just going always felt so good. In those days I could travel independently for a month on 100 pounds and want for nothing. It was $5-a-day stuff, with maybe a four-star treat once in a while. Magic Bus, Eurocity Express—simple, clean rooms without a view, unless you slept on the roof of a particular hotel or hostel where that was the only alternative when they were full, and I did sometimes, with the company of like-minded travellers around me and the stars above me. I always went by train and ferry at night; that way a comfortable sleep cost nothing extra, and you were still going somewhere new . . . like Timbuktu! Mr. Cleary, sir!

To travel like this you need patience and time; you can't package the way I moved about with unreserved abandon. I gave myself over to the gods of destiny. The trip became a daily happening, engaging me with the sacred and the profane, the calmness to the insane, the reality to the game and into the unknown, never the same, like a moth to a flame, only me to blame, the echo of the deserted silence, the wild beat of the drum. The senses united to every sensation, the freedom afforded in my next destination, the language I spoke my imagination, the songs I heard my dreams' illumination, the mistakes that I made tomorrow's inspiration . . .

On the other hand, travel with Nirvana was entirely another story. Our expenses were paid by the record company or the promoter. Flights were booked and paid for in advance. A driver was there around the clock to chauffeur us in whatever city we were playing. We had good hotels, food and drinks on room service, an allowance for our stagewear, and spending money in the local currency. (This was before the Euro replaced the French franc, the German mark and the Dutch guilder). We played in Hungary on one occasion, in a Budapest football stadium—Frank Zappa and the Mothers of Invention and it's a Beautiful Day were on the same show. We were all paid in the local currency, which was useless outside Hungary, so everyone went on a spending spree; what we had left over we gave to some kids on the road out to the airport. We started to take some control over our travelling costs when we were told later by the record company accounts department that every expenditure we incurred, including our recording costs, were deductible from our earnings, royalties included.

The money we received for a TV show and a concert in a European city never covered the expense of going there to do it. in fact, what we and any other band with a recording contract were doing was borrowing money (you never had it physically in your hands) from the record company, to promote and sell their product! They owned our recordings forever—in perpetuity is what it said in the contract—then when the royalties were earned and booking fees came in, they deducted what we owed, and paid us our agreed contractual share of the balance, if there was one. Even with our low royalty rate, though it was improved many years later with the help of a lawyer, I know for a fact that we were one of the very few acts on Island Records to be in the black when we parted company with them.

Most bands had four or five members and a

roadie; we were just two. Many bands, signed to major record companies, never even managed to pay back their recording costs, and after two or three album releases were dropped or they disbanded. Disbanded. What a defining word that was back then . . . not now. Today, one or two original members will do; bands re-form to play holiday camps, cruise ships and farewell tours—I have heard them referred to as Pension Fund Tours. Maybe we should try a comeback ourselves! "For one night only at the Albert Hall, London," with the BBC Symphony orchestra, has been suggested to us for 2009, the 40th anniversary of Nirvana U.K. But who would pay for it? Maybe it is just as beautiful and rewarding to sit on the Atlantic coastline of Morocco at Essaouira and imagine that I can hear it.

Oh yes! Morocco! Essaouira, Tangier, Casablanca, Fez, Oujda, Marrakesh, Quarzazate. I have tasted them all, and the first feast was memorable—my kind of travel, and a new kind of music. Around that time I had read *The Sheltering Sky*, written in 1949 by Paul Bowles, an American composer-writer from New York. He lived in Tangier for 20 years with his wife, Jane, an artist in her own right. They travelled regularly between Tangier and Paris, London, the USA; their circle included Allen Ginsberg, William Borroughs, Tennessee Williams, Gore Vidal, Gregory Corso, Truman Capote and Ned Rorem (an American composer whose Paris Diaries I had read). Tangier's artist colony attracted American and British bohemian types and drifters, often with inheritance money to waste on the pleasure of others. If you were part of that elite group, you could do whatever you liked in Tangier, and there were never any consequences. The inhabitants and the civil authority of the city knew of Paul and Jane's legendary excesses and the recklessness of some of their visitors, but they adopted Bowles as one of their own; their reclusive brother had the keys to the citadel. Being gay or bisexual was a garnish to one's mystique; everybody spoke French or English and knew the right words for the right occasions in Arabic—the first word I had in Arabic was *merhaba,* a good greeting.

In London, the Speakeasy and the Bag of Nails were the two membership-only clubs where all the musicians and their entourages let their hair down, shall we say. Away from the stage area, the Speakeasy had a very good restaurant, which could often be on the wild side, especially if there was a punch-up. The restaurant was where all the gossip and the deals went down. Morocco was mentioned a lot there: Brian and Keef from the Stones had driven to Morocco from Paris; Jimi Hendrix went there and found Essaouira and Brigitte Bardot!

Jimmy Miller, our Island producer, was raving about percussive ensemble music that was being made in Morocco's Atlas Mountains. He had a live cassette tape that somebody brought back and copied for him, but he would not play it for us . . . "Too precious, man." The following summer, Brian Jones and his engineer friend George Chkiantz recorded the Pan pipes of Jajouka, a town in the Rif Mountains of the northern Atlas range. Related to the Sufi tradition, the pipers' trance music is associated with healing and ritual. Maybe Jimmy Miller's cassette was from the same region? He later produced the Stones, and if you listen to *Beggars Banquet, Let it Bleed, Sticky Fingers and Exile on Main Street*, these are testimony to his talent as a producer, percussionist and drummer.

In London, a lot of the hash—or *kif* as it is called in Arabic (the word is derived from another meaning pleasure)—came from Morocco. It was a very mild smoke and soft on the throat, but you knew that if you went there, to the source, and indulged in the bongs and the hookahs (water pipes), it was going to be purer and more powerful, so you had to be careful. The Rif Mountains and their valleys was the area that produced this cash crop—some of which eventually made its way to Portobello Road and many other roads and streets in London for the pleasure of many who went there to score. Morocco via Paris was a very enticing proposition, and the Beat Hotel in the Latin Quarter of that city, a hippie meeting place for writers and poets, would maybe result in some good contacts for the onward trip and the stay in Morocco itself.

Nirvana made a number of working trips to Paris around 1968 and 1969; our records sold well there, and two of the city's best and most popular singers, Françoise Hardy and Herve Villard, covered our songs. At a café called Chopin near the Odeon Mêtro, we met up a few times with Aphrodite's Child, the Greek group that was started by Vangelis. Alex knew Vangi since their school days in Athens. The band had a deal with Philips Records but were struggling to come up with a hit or a successful sound; with a little help from Pachelbel they delivered "Rain and Tears" in 1968, and it was a biggie for them. We also had the same publisher in Paris, Maurice Boucheaux.

The Café Chopin was a hangout for students, writers, painters, musicians, freaks, agitators, beatniks and aesthetic females . . . my kind of place. It was there that I met an interesting girl from Montpellier in the South of France. She liked to travel and paint; she was married to an Algerian; he was a doctor in his hometown of Oran, a historic port on the Algerian coast near the frontier with Morocco. She kept an apartment in Montpellier, where she lived for six months of the year on her own. She invited me to come there with her. Then after a few days, the plan was to go to Marseille and catch an overnight boat to Oran. I knew that Alex had already planned to spend six weeks in Athens after our return to London, and we had scheduled early September to finish the writing and recording of our new LP.

I took up the invitation to travel with my new friend, and explained that my intention was to go on to Morocco from Oran, and she was welcome to come with me if she so desired. She told me it would be impossible, because her husband would not allow her to travel to any other African country, even French-speaking, Arabic Morocco. It was strange, I thought—he was okay with her being in France on her own for six months, but he would not accept her visiting the country next door. I decided to ask no questions and enjoy what was on offer. After a couple of days back in London to sort out our business, Alex took a flight to Athens and I took a train from Victoria to Montpellier; the Beat Hotel in Paris was given a miss. I was welcomed like a brother.

Montpellier had a great vibe about it, with the old streets and alleys, the courtyard apartments and lofts, the markets . . . it was a French Portobello Road, but the immigrant community was Algerian. Everywhere we went was run by Algerians: the restaurants, the launderette, the art centre where my friend sold and gave painting class, the cafés and bakery, and the rai music club. Rai, my first new music, smacked me in the face, punched me in the stomach and kicked me in the bollocks. I identified with it as I did with the blues of Jimmy Reed, Howlin' Wolf, Sonny Boy Williamson and other migrants from the Mississippi Delta to Chicago; I identified with it as I did with Margaret Barry, the itinerant singer from Donegal whom I had heard in London at a ballroom in Kilburn . . . Irish blues! I identified with it as I did with the signs I saw on some pubs in London that read, "No dogs, no blacks, no Irish"—it was all the blues.

I identified with rai as I did with the Sean Nós unaccompanied singing of the West of Ireland, Connemara blues . . . I identified with it because I was a migrant myself, and I felt what the Algerians were singing about in their language. Rai means to have an opinion, a voice and the freedom to express it. Its songs and words were about drinking, suicide, suffering, colonialism, poverty, exile, homesickness, corruption, copulation and lovemaking.

My friend explained it all to me: that from Algerian independence in 1962 onwards, Oran was called Little Paris, and that rai, with its origins in Algerian Berber music, was sung in the bars and bordellos of the town. Seen as subversive, provocative music, it was banned by the authorities, who used their power to enforce obedience. I was beginning to understand why there were so many Algerians in Montpellier and Paris—including my friend, even if it was only for half of the year—and why her husband had to stay in Oran. France was a place where Algerians could participate in utopian freedom: party all night if they wanted to; walk openly with your girl, hand in hand; make and be part of rai, an essential to their identity, as much as it was seductive and sexy; find a place at a university and get a degree that would take those with ambition and drive farther afield, maybe to the USA.

It was not until 1985 that the greatest exponent of rai (and a national hero in his country), Cheb Khaled, was able to return to be crowned the king of rai at its first ever festival in Oran. Cheb means "young man," chebba "young woman," and most of the singers are called by that name. Cheb Djellal, one of today's young and mighty popular singers, is based in Paris. Khaled is still king, but Djellal is the innovative young prince. In the late '50s and early '60s, the rai music in places like Oran was played on a *gasba* (a wooden flute) and a *darbouka* (the essential hand drum, like the *bindir* in Morocco and the *bodhran* in Ireland). All *darboukas* are made from the unblemished skin of a white goat—for the best sound, they say. Was Mr. Cleary on the ball when he told us it was highly possible Arab sailors came up the Atlantic as far as the west coast of Ireland—maybe Kerry or Galway—en route from North Africa to Spain (Gallicia) and Brittany in France!! I have seen with my own eyes fishermen in the Red Sea using a boat (tar-covered hide on wooden slats) with the one-paddle, one-net hand technique . . . It's exactly the same as the single *currach* boat used by fishermen from the wild western coast of my own country.

With the hand drum and wooden flute, there were also violins in the rai groups. Cheb Khaled brought in guitars and synthesizers and dropped the violins to give it a shot of rock and roll. He was a big fan of Johnny Hallyday and Elvis, and was prepared to take on that mantle in the new rai that swept France. Latter-day rai has been exploited by the record industry and assimilated into the amorphous genre called world music. Cheb Djellal mixes rai and reggae, so that is another approach with a world influence, but for me, rai is Algerian blues; jab, gnawa, and jilala are Moroccan blues; Sean Nós is Irish blues; and the field songs, prison songs and spirituals of slavery from America's South are the blues . . . but it all came out of Africa.

I knew before we set out from Marseille that Oran

was not going to have the open, lively vibrancy that was Montpellier. It was not comfortable there, and I knew I would not be staying long, though my hosts were polite and did everything to make it an interesting time for me. Her husband had his own driver to take him to and from a central medical building in the town centre; the house was right by the Mediterranean shoreline; they had a full-time live-in maid/housekeeper who was from the capital, Algiers. Everything was timed and planned by her husband, who was speaking French to his wife, English to me and Arabic to the housekeeper and driver, often in the same conversation. He was in his early 50s; his wife was 27; the housekeeper was about the same age; the driver was her uncle. The area where they lived was an exclusive zone, regularly patrolled by military security personnel.

I was not the first male acquaintance that my friend had brought back from France; it seemed that every time she returned she was accompanied by "an artistic type of person" (that's how her husband described them) who "sometimes are with us for months." Her husband wore a different polo-neck sweater for each of the three days I stayed; in Paris and Montpellier his wife wore her free spirit every day, but in Oran she wore, as it were, a mask. On one of the six balconies round the house, they set up a hammock—not any old hammock; this was straight out of Persia, embroidered in silk with velvet patches, in radiant colours, and matching cushions around and underneath; if you rolled out, you would never know it! Fit for a pasha from the Orient or a Berber warlord . . . this was where I slept. We made three excursions, all by car—to the fortress and harbour area, to the best restaurant in Oran, which was on the ocean, and to an open-air cinema.

My friend's husband asked me on the way back from the cinema, in perfect English pronunciation, "Do you know any of the great English train robbers?" The film that we had seen was *Le Balcon*, from a novel by the French writer Jean Genet. He told me that Genet loved criminals and homosexuals and had been a vagabond travelling across Europe, something he would have liked to have done himself. He said the film could have been about people he knew; it is set in a brothel where the clients could be politically powerful people—or are they pretending to be, or is what we see just reflections in mirrors . . . ?

I decided I was moving into Morocco the next day and enquired about the easiest way to get to the frontier at Oujda. My friend's husband decided that their driver would take me there and that his wife would accompany me "to the frontier only," and he smiled. The frontier had six sections: three on the Algerian side and three on the Moroccan, and my Irish passport was treated as an interesting curiosity at every section. As on the Zambesi . . . I sailed through. The Irish passport is the only one in the world that has a musical instrument, the harp, as its emblem . . . it speaks for itself . . . and I can hear the music.

At the taxi and camel station in Oujda, I met Honey and Spice. They told me their father worked as a driver at the Coca-Cola plant; their mother was doing time for stealing her sister's baby! In Oujda, everyone worked for Coca-Cola at the North African distribution centre, which dwarfed the town of "breeze-block boxes"—the workers' houses!—all of which seemed to be connected to aerials and pylons that were on the roof of the massive plant. It looked as if Coca-Cola had a generator that was supplying electric power to everybody in the town, including the Chinese restaurant on the dusty main street. There were also these secretive-looking office shops—the best way I can describe them—that displayed typewriters next to coffee beans, empty vodka bottles and photo albums with plastic flowers strewn around them. The street led to a sweltering stand for Mercedes taxis, and for dozens of camels and their handlers, who were resting before going into the baking desert. Many of the handlers wore Coca-Cola baseball caps, as did a few of the camels. One of the taxi drivers told me that there were hundreds of Chinese working in the area on long-term infrastructure energy and plant-construction projects. Coca-Cola was the only employer in Oujda, as far as I could see.

In Mandarin, Coca-Cola means "delicious happiness."

In Oujda, Coca-Cola means everything.

The Mercedes taxi boys operated from Oujda to Meknes, there and back (if you were coming back!), six persons to a taxi, including the driver—maybe seven, if the weight of the six had not pushed the chassis too close to the ground. It was $5 one way, but you had to wait until the driver had the full load for the dusty, bumpy, musk-odourous, non-air-conditioned drive across the desert.

It made no difference if you paid the driver the full $25 and hired him exclusively; he would take your money, disappear for a few hours, arrive back shouting and quarreling with his brothers in Arabic, and still wait for another four people. It was all a game—a pantomime in the desert—and the foreigner, the visitor, was the fall guy. I was the only person in the taxi not wearing a *djellaba.* I had my passport, documents and dollars in a well-hidden pouch pocket inside of my trouser front, and that's where they were going to stay. Honey and Spice were looking out for me on the trip, smiling and asking me in French if I was okay. They all spoke Arabic for about an hour, then fell asleep, snoring on each other's shoulders. I saw the driver's head drop on his chest a number of times, but the Mercedes, moving like a tank, always hit something on the desert road, and he soon realised he was at the wheel of his "daily bread." I did not sleep, because I feared someone would try to get inside my pants for my passport and dollars, and Honey and Spice might even be in on the plot. I knew that these people would not harm me, but if I gave them the chance, they might rob me. When we reached Meknes that evening, Honey and Spice said their goodbyes;

they were going to Bir-Tam-Tam. Just before they left, Honey turned to me and said, "Our brother 'Temptation' will be waiting for you at the bus station in Tangier . . . he knows you are coming."

The brothers and sisters of Temptation are all over Morocco; as soon as you arrive out of a bus depot, train station or taxi halt, they are waiting for you. They watch and study you from a distance, undressing you with their eyes, then they make their moves on you. Women did not travel alone in Morocco then, and many would still not today unless with an official government-approved guide. Couples, yes, but the brothers and sisters of Temptation might try to separate you . . . just like in *The Sheltering Sky*. On the advice of another taxi driver at Meknes, who spoke excellent English (he was married to an American woman who was a Muslim and a religious ceramic artist; they had met in Istanbul), I was to take the overnight bus to Tangier, where I could spend a few days and then ride the train, the Marrakesh Express, even though it meant going north, away from my destination in the southwest. The massive Atlas Mountains stood in the way of the shorter route.

On the bus, which also served as a bed, everyone

slept with their *djellaba* hoods pulled up snugly around their heads; many stretched out on their belongings over two seats. The elderly man who sat in front of me, wearing a white *djellaba*, spoke to me in Arabic; he had no teeth. I realised that he was an imam—a holy man! a priest! a scholar! For most of the journey, he chanted very softly a prayer, a mantra. I listened to his music and watched the most incredible starry sky; then I was crying for no reason I could understand.

Temptation, no more than 16 years old, was waiting for me when I came out of the Tangier bus depot. The place was a hive of activity—luminous people in vivid colours; *tadjeen* cooking smells and spiced aromas; a walking, waking mass of male sexual dynamic, and not a woman in sight. Arabs, Berbers and blacks made up most of Morocco's 25 million population, and they all seemed to be here, in red *tarbouche* (hat from Fez) and *kaftan* (a *djellaba* without a hood)—street sellers, shoe shiners, flute players, soldiers, settlers, inhabitants, sultans, casbah fakirs, and imams (my fellow passenger was welcomed with a bowing of the head and a palm of the hand on the chest by a group of holy men also in white *djellabas*).

To Temptation I made it clear and understood that I wanted to stay in the *medina* (market) area, and I asked him to take me there. His broken English, babbling on the way, went . . . "Me friend, you best hotel, you happy, me happy! Tangier very good! You Englees man! Me go for many Englees friend, breakfast, very good hotel. He my brother" (every time a boy of his own age joined us on the street). If they got too close to me, he swore at them in Arabic and spat in the street. He took me to the "lost hotel"—walled inside the main walls of the medina and situated in a glade of tall palm trees and oriental shrubs. It was the perfect oasis, with birdsong in the garden and sub-Saharan *gimbri* (lute) music in the reception area, which was totally covered in *zellige* (Moroccan mosaic).

I gave Temptation his payment—a dollar—and he left me with the words, "Me many dollar, go America." My room was all fabric, wooden marquetry, mosaic and stone inlay. The bed was a three-poster—one post had been removed, for no reason that I could imagine, and I have a good imagination. The door was heavy carved oak with a discreet heart-shaped peephole in a sculpted silver plate. In an otherworldly, hypnotic tiredness, I slept till I was wakened early the next morning by the call to prayer from the mosque in the *medina* . . . had I dreamt that someone was pounding on my door during the night? Had I dreamt that I got up and looked through the peephole to see a nomadic black man wearing a cowboy hat and boots, with a druggy-eyed, miniskirted blonde Lolita in his grip? Had I dreamt that he smacked her across the face and pushed her up close to the door and started pounding with his fist again, even harder than the first time? Dream or reality? That's how it was in Tangier for the two weeks I stayed at the "lost hotel," adventuring into the *medina* and other areas of the city, from where on higher ground you could see the coastline of Spain across the Straits of Gibraltar.

Had I dreamt that I met Moulay, a merchant from Larache, a harbour town above Tangier, and his three daughters (or were they his younger sisters!)? Had I dreamt that I was entertained by them at his *dar* (a house in the *medina*), where they stayed when they came into Tangier, and that I was his guest at a party he gave for his son's circumcision ritual? Had I dreamt that he offered me the hand of any of his three daughters in marriage? Had I dreamt that as I came out of the hotel one night, Temptation was waiting for me, sitting in the lotus position by the lily pond? Had I dreamt that he took me to the "temple" (I thought it would be an ancient site or building in the *medina*), where I found myself in a gay vodka bar in the basement of a store that sold cassettes of Moroccan dance music? What was playing on the PA system was ritualistic and erotic; it slid around you like a snake, pulling you into its rhythmic trance; your desire to dance was overpowering, and you succumbed to its *lila* . . . Wonderful if I had been with a woman, but as men have never turned me on, its passion was wasted on me. Had I dreamt that I saw Jimi Hendrix and Brigitte Bardot walking together in the *medina*?

Had I dreamt that I met Geronimo from Georgia (not USA but USSR, as it was then)? He had been in Morocco for 15 years, "trekking, trucking and fucking!" and regularly took wealthy groups of travellers into the desert at Quarzazate. Geronimo had a tattoo of a zebra on his penis, which he took out to show his travellers if they chipped in a dollar each; it was his "party piece around the campfire" on their first night together, and he had a zebra story to go with it. Had I dreamt that

I dressed up in a psychedelic silk shirt and white linen trousers and went to the Café Hafa, which overlooked the Atlantic, where the sunsets were spectacular? Had I dreamt that Paul and Jane Bowles were sitting there with some very official consulate type, a man in a dark pinstripe suit and spats? They were placed at a table where they could see everything that was happening in the room, and a professional group of musicians—violin, lute, fiddle and zither—were playing background village music that had been adapted for the town. Nobody disturbed the Bowles' table . . .

Had I dreamt that I met people who had arrived from different parts of the world to this place of debauched charm? Some came in search of pleasure, knowledge, adventure; others to find solutions to inner conflicts; others for the drums, the dance and the *kif*. Had I dreamt that in one of the *souks* of the *medina* I paid $5 for a *rabab* (one-string fiddle) and $5 more for a cassette tape of ritual music that the seller convinced me would ward off any evil spirits?

Had I dreamt that I heard whispering voices outside my door again, and that smoke was coming into the room? I went quietly to peep, my heart racing, and I could see Cowboy and his whore outside; he was smoking a joint, then going down on his knees to blow the smoke from his mouth into my room under the door. They waited around outside for ten minutes, then he pounded the door with his fist and put his face up against the peephole; all I could see was a big evil eye. They turned around and swaggered down the hall; I pulled a heavy chest of drawers across my door and went back to bed . . . to dream once more. I dreamt of Onyx from Boston, whom I had met in the *medina* a few days earlier. We drank mint tea together and had a smoke on the hookah. She had been travelling the hippie trail since she could remember.

I woke up with the realisation that I was not going to Marrakesh. In fact, I needed to make a supreme effort just to get out of Tangier . . . and Morocco!

I checked out after the morning coffee and walked through the *medina* with my bags. Temptation appeared suddenly from nowhere and wanted to help me carry them. I refused, gave him a dollar and told him to fuck off, which he understood. In reply he gave me the knife across-the-throat sign with his hand and disappeared into the *souks.* The taxi stand was on the other side of the *medina.* I got there by the main street, which I knew well by now, took a taxi to the port, made the short ferry ride across the strait to Algeciras, Spain, and was on that night's train to Paris. I was back in London three days later.

It was 15 years before I returned to Morocco—to Marrakesh in 1982—and my most recent visit there in early 2008 was my tenth. Yes, it has changed a lot, but it still has that edge, that fascination, that hunter instinct, as in Brazil, Haiti, Cuba, where you want to go deeper into things, but you always know when to back off or move on, without hurting anyone's feelings or disrespecting their culture . . . And I still have the travel and the music in me. Geographical respect, Mr. Cleary, sir!

Indulgent Recommendation for the iPod Generation

Cheb Djellal, *Le Prince de la Chanson Maghrebine*

Ned Rorem (composer, writer):

***The String Symphony, Sunday Morning* and *Eagles* (Grammy Award-winning recording, Atlanta Symphony Orchestra, 1989)**

***End of Summer* and *Book of Hours* (chamber music, Bright Music, download from www.classicsonline.com)**

RIO DE JANEIRO WITH JIMMY CLIFF
1968

Jimmy Cliff was born on April Fools' Day 1948, but believe me he is nobody's fool. He is one of the wisest and most spiritual of persons that I have had the pleasure to meet and travel with in music, and is a great songwriter. We met at Island's first office in Oxford Street London in late 1967, just as Nirvana was sprouting wings and nearly ready to fly, and Jimmy was considering a flight home to St. Catherine's in Jamaica. He was homesick, and frustrated with Island Records—he felt he was being left behind, not a priority in the overall plan that was gaining momentum under Chris Blackwell's new signings such as Nirvana, Traffic, Spooky Tooth, Fairport Convention and Free. It was very much a group situation, and Jimmy, as a solo artist, was a fish out of water.

Jimmy kept writing and demoing his songs, playing them in the office to everyone who was around, including Chris, but for the most part he was getting negative feedback. It was not that the songs were average, but they lacked a direction, a spark, a production vibe. As Jimmy Miller would say, his message was not coming through on tape. Maybe London was not right for his spirit. The passion burned in his eyes, but it was not going to the recordings that he was creating, even though he had a voice gifted from God. Still, however he felt inside, he always had a loving smile on his face outside.

Jimmy became quite attached to Alex and me: Like him, we were away from our native lands. We also understood and felt his need of friendship and support, and we gave it unconditionally. We went along to hear him sing one night with Herbie Goins and the Nighttimers, who played good, solid soul-funk. Their brass section, led by a sax player, Mick Eve, was the best in the business, and was doing lots of session work with other recording groups during the day and playing live every night; the horn men were a well-drilled and well-turned outfit, and they could all "read the dots." Jimmy, live on stage, was a revelation; he was able to deliver what was missing in his recordings, and I realised that night he had the star quality that would make him a success in the not-too-distant future. The passion I had seen in his eyes I now saw onstage, as did the rest of the audience. The talent was there, and he was a consummate professional. He had prepared himself for this "might happen, might not happen" spot on the show with Herbie and the Nighttimers as he would have for the top of the bill in Las Vegas. His stagewear was immaculate, and he sparkled all over, with moves and steps that had been well worked out in the mirror. I told him what I felt about his performance after the show, but he was on an emotional high; his roller coaster was still turning, and he may not have really taken in what I said.

Back at Island HQ, as the weeks went by, Jimmy was still waiting in limbo for Chris to launch him with a record. He became despondent and worried about his situation in London. Like the rest of us, he had to find money to survive and pay his way. He had a sister who lived in the Wembley area, and he stayed with her for some months. I don't know what arrangement Jimmy had with Chris about money and support, but I knew he was not on a salary like ourselves and the other bands, because he was never there on a Friday to be paid like the rest of us. I felt that Chris and Jimmy were not able to work out the crossover from the Jamaican music to the progressive/psychedelic rock that Island was innovating, and their relationship was floundering. Whatever Chris saw in him when Jimmy represented Jamaica at the World's Trade Fair in New York two years earlier was not working out in London. Jimmy was down but not out, and I did not see him for about a month . . . Then fate played its hand for both of us.

A few months before this, I had written a song called "Waterfall" with Alex, and Jimmy was the vocalist on the demo—we paid him a session fee from our budget. The song was not for a Nirvana LP, but we had it orchestrated for strings and brass, and managed to get it done at the end of one of our own sessions. (We used to call those recordings "something for the bottom drawer" or "Israeli bombs"; we just put them away until the right time in the future.) It was a commercial song and a master-quality recording, with a good performance from Jimmy; we gave him an acetate copy for his own collection of works.

What I did not know was that Jimmy played it to Elsa, the P.A. to Chris Blackwell, and she, using her initiative and intuition, sent it to the organisers of the Rio de Janeiro (Brazil) International Song Festival . . . I had never heard of it before. I believe she was spurred on by Jimmy's sense of rejection and her own inner motivation to help him, whatever! Her shot in the dark was to change his life forever. I went into the office to meet with Jimmy Miller about some mixes he was doing with our songs. Elsa called me over to her desk and in a very casual, laid-back voice said, "Patrick, would you like to go to Rio de Janeiro, all expenses paid?" It was like being asked to be the first Irish astronaut to go to the moon! By an amazing stroke of luck, Jimmy Cliff had been selected by the festival organisers to represent Jamaica, singing our song "Waterfall." I was shocked and elated, and excited for Jimmy. I started to laugh about it when I said to Elsa, "This is unreal—a song written by an Irishman and a Greek will represent Jamaica, the land of reggae, in Brazil, the land of samba."

"What about Alex?" I said. "Have you told him?" He was in Athens at the time. Elsa had told him, and as fate would have it there also, he had decided to stay longer in Greece, and the one-ticket-only composer representation (rules of the festival) was mine; there would be no need to toss a coin for this experience of a lifetime.

I met Jimmy and his treasured acoustic guitar at Heathrow Airport. I could not believe the amount of luggage he had. As well as suitcases and bags, he had a trunk that opened out like a small wardrobe to reveal at least ten stage suits and shirts hanging neatly, and on the lower level, the same number of pairs of Cuban-heel boots, shining and ready to dance. I knew in that instant that Jimmy would not be coming back to London with me when the festival was over.

Our flight was with Lufthansa, the German airline, and at its desk a representative of the British Music Publishers Association and his wife, and a representative of the Brazilian Consulate in London and his wife (well, they introduced them as their wives), welcomed us and informed us that the flight was originating in Frankfurt, where the German and Scandinavian singers and writers were boarding; it then proceeded to London Heathrow for the English representative and ourselves (the Jamaican entry . . . that still makes me smile after all those years), then to Lisbon, where Portugal, Spain, Italy, France and Israel—maybe!—would join the flight. (The Israeli singer, who had written his own song, had just been called up to fight in the Six Day War, and nobody knew if he was going to make it or not.) Then it was party on down to Rio. I was positive Jimmy's guitar would make an appearance on the flight . . . and I was not wrong.

The English singer Anita Harris arrived with her manager and her husband and was introduced all round. A successful pop ballad recording artist and the choice to represent England, she was giving it all the "I'm a star, don't come too close" treatment as were her two peacocks, opening every door and kissing every floor before she took a step. Conversely, Jimmy and I came across as two convivial buskers. At Lisbon we were joined by the French singer Françoise Hardy and the others, about whom I had not a clue other than that they were stars in their own countries. When the Israeli singer-songwriter appeared onboard with minutes to spare, everyone cheered and clapped, and the party started. A Carnival atmosphere took over the flight; we danced the samba at 40,000 feet above the Atlantic. Jimmy's guitar was in demand, and the Israeli singer was at the centre of the sing-along for most of the way—understandably so, as a few days earlier he was fighting a war.

On our arrival at Rio de Janeiro airport, the flashbulbs started popping on the press photographers' cameras; TV newspeople had set up to film our arrival; the British ambassador to Brazil and festival committee people were there in linen suits and silk cravats, looking very colonial. Jimmy, never one to miss an opportunity, headed straight for the hundreds of cheering, smiling Brazilian music fans, shaking their hands and giving them hugs while still looking like a Carnival busker. I don't think any of us realised how big a deal the festival was in Brazil—it had blanket coverage on TV and radio every night and was front page in all the newspapers. The organisation was first-class in every sense: A motorcade, escorted by police on Harley-Davidsons, took us from the airport to the best hotel in town, the Copacabana on the beach in the centre of the city, with Ipanema to the right and Christ the Redeemer and the Sugar Loaf Mountain above us to the left. The staff allocated to each country all spoke three or four languages fluently and were there around the clock to advise us and take us on prearranged tours. The festival itself was a riot of songs, fireworks, joy and celebration, building up over the week to the final night and gala concert.

On the first four nights, concerts were broadcast live on TV to find the song that would represent Brazil. This was a brilliant piece of organisation on the part of the committee, creating a passion and a fervour throughout Brazil, and especially Rio, that would continue to the final international night. Everybody had a favourite singer and song; the support was overwhelming. All the international guests were invited to the final show, where the Brazilian song would be chosen from a combination of votes, audience reaction and TV response. The favourite was a song that had captured the public's imagination because its lyric took a lethal swipe at the country's leadership and some of its dictatorial policies.

The crowd whooped and cheered and sang the song with the singer all through his performance, which was accompanied only by his acoustic guitar playing. Everyone in Brazil knew the song; it had been on TV three nights running and stood out from many of the other entries, which were samba or romantic pop. When it was chosen—after much deliberation, to the annoyance of the packed open-air auditorium—the place broke out in firecrackers that lit the night; smoke enveloped the arena.

Brazil celebrates like no other country in the world; being there feels like being on the edge of a volcano about to erupt. It never lets up, from the sacred celebration of women kneeling at Virgin statues set in the middle of flower-surrounded roundabouts smack in the middle of the highways, to the celebration of taxi drivers joyous to inform you that there are only three important things in their lives: football first, religion next, and finally the family.

Brazilian football is a wild theatre of sport. As part of the international representation, we were invited to a match at the world-famous Maracana Stadium, the biggest in the world; its capacity then was 200,000, since reduced for safety. The night we went, it was packed to the burning rafters. It was like being in a Fellini epic—a Dante's Inferno of smoke, deafening noise and flashing fire; passion and pride ran as high as the fireworks that lit the dusky sky. Botafogo was the most popular team in Rio at that time; the others were Flamengo (the most popular team today) and Fluminese, the sworn enemy of both.

That night Botafogo was playing Santos, from the state of São Paulo. Santos was a city 75 kilometres up the coast from São Paulo city itself, but most important, it was the team that Pele captained and played for. Garraincha was the captain of Botafogo; both of them were stars on the Brazilian National Team, and Jimmy, however he managed it, was introduced with some other festival luminaries to both of them on the centre circle before the match began. He had told me when he arrived earlier to our reserved festival-guest seats that he might have to do an interview, and disappeared into the crowd. It was a great photo opportunity for him, and he made the major newspapers next morning . . . the boy was flying.

The stadium exploded into the night when Pele scored what I believed was the winning goal, but the papers the next morning said it was a 1-1 draw; his goal had been disallowed. In the confusion of colour, smoke, spectacle, athleticism, and football (ballet with the moves of chess, swagger and samba . . . yes, the footballers danced samba as they played), the result was not conclusive; there remained a mystery hanging over the Night of the Maracana. That's the way it felt to me as a first-time visitor, and the experience was unforgettable. Football was Brazil's religion (and still is today, I believe), and I had been to its greatest cathedral. I was a witness, and my testimony to what I believe they call "the beautiful game" is this written memory. It is indelible.

The next morning Jimmy told me that the Righteous Brothers and Paul Anka had arrived at the hotel; they were to represent the USA and Canada respectively, and one of the TV programmes had an interview with Jay Livingstone and Ray Evans, the American songwriters whose compositions included the standards "Que Será Será" ("Whatever Will Be Will Be"), "Mona Lisa" and "Buttons and Bows." They were the festival guests of honour and members of the international panel of judges . . . this really was the big league.

At the hotel, Jimmy and I had adjoining rooms that had a sliding partition, which we often left open; I was aware that Jimmy prayed quite often, always on his knees, which was how I prayed myself as a young boy before I went to bed each night. During those memorable days together, he played me some of the new songs he had been writing over the previous despondent months in London; they were still taking shape, but he had taken his songwriting to another level. "Many Rivers to Cross" and "Sitting Here in Limbo" (the "here" was dropped later) were the two he endlessly played and worked on, and I was convinced he had cracked it big-time. I remember saying, "Jimmy, I think you have written two standards," and I was definitely proved right on one of them—"Many Rivers to Cross" has become a reggae classic worldwide and has been recorded by Joe Cocker and UB40, and John Lennon produced a version for Harry Nilsson. "Sitting Here in Limbo" was covered by Jerry Garcia, David Grisman, Willie Nelson and Fiona Apple.

I knew that both songs had come out of the

frustrations and setbacks Jimmy had experienced in London, "Sitting Here in Limbo" especially so. "Many Rivers to Cross" is a spiritually searching song about having belief in oneself and in a God who is good, never losing hope in Him. We did not discuss religion. I knew from the beginning that he had the faith, as I did, though at that time I was going through a difficult period, which lasted a decade, of analytical opposition to Catholicism because of the indoctrination and abuse that I had been through into my late teens at the hands of of the Christian Brothers. I did not know if Jimmy was Catholic, Baptist, Adventist; I just knew he prayed and believed in a God. He knew I was Catholic; he had asked me, "Are all the Irish Catholic, the same as yourself?" And when he first met us, Alex had explained to him the basic beliefs of the Greek Orthodox Church. Jimmy was a believer and a seeker; many of his songs over the following years have come from that source of inspiration.

God was surely on our side the night we went to the School of Samba in one of the safe neighbourhoods of the city. Samba schools started in Rio in 1928 and have evolved around the centrepiece event of the Rio

Carnival. There are many in the city, and they are the home bases for the floats, costumes and drummers that practise and prepare all year for the Greatest Show on Earth. However, on most nights you could go to a samba school that took pace in an open playground area or a big yard. Some were oriented towards the tourism business; others had an edge and a genuine atmosphere of unpredictability. And if you were accompanied, as we were, by a local, it was safe to go there and samba all night to the hot, erotic rhythms of the drums, ten in a row, ten deep; when the front line needed a break from the action, they moved to the back line, and so it went on. Sellers with small freezers strapped to their backs moved through the swaying crowd, the only drink available cold beer from the bottle.

Our host girl from Rio (South zone) organised a visit to one of the real, lively samba schools for a group that included Jimmy and myself, the singers and writers from Germany and Italy, and our Israeli friend, who was becoming a bit of a celebrity in the papers and on television, as his story appealed to the public. The sound level in a samba school never drops, just as in the football stadiums, the *favellas*, the beaches, the streets—it's a continuous wave of drums, tambourines, rattles, crackers and fireworks. In that trippy and trancelike atmosphere, about 500 people were on the samba floor, including our group in the thick of it all . . . it was like being in a voodoo village.

Then there was the familiar sound of firecrackers going off—maybe three or four rapid bangs, then two or three more in succession, by which time people around us were throwing themselves on the floor, falling under each other, on top of each other, pulling others down with them, which instinctively we did ourselves in those panic moments of realisation that it was gunshots we were hearing, and it was all kicking off only yards away. Out of somewhere and within seconds, two police riders on Harleys came through the parting crowd, sirens wailing. There was screaming and crying as people carried others away; one body was being dragged along by its feet. None of our group was hurt; it had all happened in seconds. The drummers did not stop playing, the samba continued on, the people danced on . . . it was a hothouse of contradiction that was impossible for an outsider to comprehend. We left shortly after the incident, and on the way back to the hotel our host told us that a jealous man who had drunk too much pulled a gun on a man he knew—shot him because that man was dancing too provocatively with his woman. As the crowd jumped to get the gun away, he shot indiscriminately at those around him. One man died, and four others had serious bullet wounds. Neither Jimmy nor I mentioned the incident again.

Over the next two days, all the international artists and songwriters were on rehearsal call for Saturday's gala finale, and we did not leave the hotel. There were two rehearsals for each act—one a test run to sort out all the technical stuff, and one full on with the orchestra. Jimmy decided that I should be onstage with him doing backing vocals, which took me by surprise. He said it made him feel good if we were there together, and he wanted to introduce me to the audience as one of the songwriters.

Come the night, it was like being back at the Maracana all over again. The concert-hall atmosphere was electric—crowds had queued all day to see the artists arriving; the show itself was sold out. Rio's social elite were in evening dress, and all the embassies and consulates in the city were represented.

For the obvious reasons, none of the artists wanted to follow the Brazilian song. I don't remember who eventually did, but it was not Jimmy. The running order ran alphabetically; he would follow the Israeli song and precede the Righteous Brothers, which was an excellent position, audiencewise. In the dressing room, we could hear the pandemonium the Brazilian song had inspired, and the Israeli song also got a massive reception. Then it was, "Representing Jamaica, Jimmy Cliff, with the song 'Waterfall,'" which was repeated in Portuguese, and the roar went up. As the orchestra played the opening bars and we ran on across the stage, I took my position with the two singers from the band; Jimmy grabbed the microphone off the stand and went into his performance. He was magical, a man possessed; he had the already-excited crowd in the palm of his hand within the first verse, and when the song went into the first key change, he did a spinning shuffle that could have easily started a riot. He repeated it twice towards the end of the song and finished off with a James Brown split, perfectly executed . . . and the song was good, too! Jimmy received a standing ovation. We watched the rest of the show on the backstage television monitors, including the Righteous Brothers, who were in a different league than everybody else, immaculate and dynamic. They had brought their own rhythm section and incorporated it into the orchestra band, and what voices . . .

The judging panel awarded Jimmy Best Performance of the Festival; he received a cash prize in U.S. dollars and went back onstage for his presentation to a rapturous ovation. The Righteous Brothers won the Festival Gold Medal and cash prize for Best Song, and the Israeli singer received a special award just for being there, as his country was at war. Paul Anka received the songwriter award. It was all a bit confusing, really, like Santos and Botafogo at the Maracana earlier in the week, but that beautiful confusion is all part of the Brazilian way. Everybody wins! Who cares? We were there and we won! The papers added to the confusion: Some had Jimmy Cliff as the winner, others the Righteous Brothers, and many said the Brazilian song had won. It had, but only the Brazilian-song part of the festival. Jimmy's Wikipedia entry says he was the winner, but seriously, it was an international song festival, and the Gold Medal winners were the Righteous Brothers representing the USA.

After the celebration party and a few hours' sleep, everything happened very quickly. Jimmy did a press interview day and a TV show in Rio on that night. The next day he flew to São Paulo to do a week of television and radio and some live appearances. We said our goodbyes, and I did not see him again until 15 years later, when he invited me to a show he did at Brixton Academy. By then he was a movie star (*The Harder they Come*, 1972) and a world-famous singer and songwriter. He had also converted to Islam in 1974. Our meeting again was a joyous occasion, but it was "allocated time," if you see what I mean. The people around him who looked after him were also Brothers of Islam, and they arranged and screened his visitors, so I had 15 minutes of private time with him in his dressing room after the show . . . that was enough time to say the things that mattered.

After the festival in Rio de Janeiro, I discovered that my return ticket on Lufthansa Airlines lacked a date and a route to London. I contacted our host girl, who managed to get me a Lufthansa flight to London via Dakar in West Africa (now Senegal), connecting to Frankfurt and London for the next day. The stopover in Dakar was colourful—oven-hot but uneventful—whereas the final Frankfurt-to-London ride was surreal.

There were only five passengers—myself and four American soldiers in their full military uniforms on their way home from the war in Vietnam; they were partying, just as our Israeli pal had on the flight out two weeks before. I was invited to their celebration, as were the cabin crew. At London's Heathrow, in a somewhat intoxicated state for early morning, I was the sole exiting arrival as the plane took on its full quota of passengers for the flight to America. It took me a week to recover, then Nirvana started our recording sessions. Rio de Janeiro (Brazil) stayed in my passport. It was only two or three years later that the importance of the trip to Rio with Jimmy became clear.

Chris Blackwell told me that Jimmy became a successful recording star and live act in Brazil, and on a short visit home to Jamaica about six months after the Festival of Rio, he met Cat Stevens; it was not planned. Stevens played him "Wild World," which Jimmy incorporated into his "Wonderful World Beautiful People," and this was the breakthrough international hit that took Jimmy to worldwide success. Brazil had been the stepping stone, "Waterfall" the calling card; Jimmy had found his rightful place. Chris Blackwell was about to find Bob Marley, and Nirvana found "All of Us" . . . Were it not for the Greek and the Irishman and darling Elsa and the "Waterfall" at the River of January, how many different rivers might Jimmy have had to cross?

Indulgent Recommendation for the iPod Generation

Bola Sete, *Voodoo Village* (Fantasy/Prestige, originally recorded in the early 1960s)

Elis Regina (with Antonio Carlos Jobim), Elis and Tom (1974)

Jimmy Cliff, "Waterfall"/"Wonderful World, Beautiful People" (1968)

FUCKING AROUND IN BELGIUM
Belgian Music Television, Simon Dupree, Ferre Grignard, 1968-69

"Belgium is a fucking weird place man!" I heard Alex shouting to me from the balcony of our hotel as I lay in bed, still stoned and hung over from the night before. "I fucking hate it!" he yelled. "Let's get out of this pisshole!" The way I was feeling, I fucking hated everywhere and anywhere, and I wanted to go nowhere.

I rolled myself off the bed and onto the faded, threadbare carpet, crawling across the room towards the open French window and out to the balcony; it was massive, twice the size of the room I slept in. I could not see Alex! "Where the fuck are you, man?" I stood up, naked as the morning but feeling like shit, and realised we had connecting rooms courtesy of the neoclassical builder, who had stuck this monstrosity of columned stone on the front of this so-called four-star hotel in the central square of Brussels, "an Island of Flems in a sea of Walloons."

French and Flemish, Wallys and Walloons, bicycles with trolleys, Dutch banjos, Stella Artois beer, boiled cabbage, sausage and dumplings—but no one smiled; there was no colour; it was a grey fucking place with ugly, unpronounceable names on the signposts, and our hotel smelt of stale piss. You could feel it was in the plumbing inside the ancient walls, like the chamber pots that were probably still under the beds. And the guy who was coming to the hotel in an hour's time to take us to the TV show—even *he* had a dodgy name.

Hans Kustard was the local publisher who was going to promote our new single release in the Benelux Territory, which was made up of Belgium, the Netherlands and Luxembourg, but the only fucking territory I wanted to be in at that moment was Slumberland, and Alex had already gone back there, the sheet over his head, singing, "I want more whiskey, and tell Belgium I'm not fucking in!" to the tune of the French National anthem, the "Elysee."

Since we arrived in this weird place, I had felt that nobody spoke to anybody else; they did not like themselves or their surroundings; their facial expression was a confused and sour stare. There was a morbid veil of mist hanging over the place, secretive and maybe sinister if you were to stumble across its source, fucking spooked or what! Maybe it was the long, dark winter nights facing the rain and winds of the North Sea. Or was it an identity thing, a geographical conundrum: Who the fuck are we? Belgian, French, Flemish, Flatlanders, Vikings, Normans, Walloons, Dutch? A colonial past and a decaying grandeur echoed in this cultural backwater with its dull agricultural landscapes . . . and where were the cosmopolitans?

Hans Kustard told us he was Dutch, I think! I was not really with it when he hammered on our hotel room doors and managed to get us out of there and into his wagon. It was a mystery to me how he did it, and he had been to the Central Station overnight luggage office to pick up our props, which were on the back seat: my angel wings and Alex's Mini-Moog, "the symptomatic stimulator." What a Dutch diamond he was!

"What's happening now?" Alex asked. "We go for

the breakfast now." I felt that I was going to throw up Technicolour, and according to Alex, I had gone a whiter shade of pale. Hans must have been well used to the antics of bands and musicians, because from somewhere on his person he produced two small bottles of black liquid that tasted of licorice. Disgusting, but it did the trick; in fact, it did the job so well that we had another bottle each. The label on these miniatures for massive hangovers read, "Frenet Branca."

Having received our much-needed digestive kick-start, we settled for coffee and coffee!! en route and started to focus on the job at hand. Kustard told us we would be the second of four acts to be filmed that day, and the show was going out the following night, a regular Saturday-night variety special, which meant we would be miming our vocals to the backing track, and generally just fucking around in front of the camera, giving some kind of resemblance to what was happening in the music; it was the standard practise of those days.

I decided to ask Hans about his name after I explained to him what custard was in England and Ireland, and how much I liked the stuff as a kid. He explained that his name was Küsters, not Kustard, with the accent on the "Kü" but as far as we were concerned I knew he would always be Kustard with the accent on the "tar," and so it was, for that trip and during the following years, he was always Hans Kustard.

"How come that a Dutch man in Belgium has the same name as the fucking general who fought at the Little Bighorn?" I asked him. He looked at me over the top of his spectacles as if I were some kind of strange plant, stopped the wagon and started to convulse with laughter and coughing. I gave Alex the nod, and we whipped our trousers down and stuck our naked arses against the windows, and Belgium was watching, but still no one smiled. Hans finally regained his composure but lost it again when we stuck the angel wings out of the wagon windows. In any other country we would have been arrested, but here all we got was indifference. I'd hate to have to earn my living as a standup comedian in that fucking place, I thought to myself.

The other three acts on the show, all London-based like ourselves, were Paul & Barry Ryan, who were riding high with "Eloise," Simon Dupree & the Big Sound, who were flying high with "Kites," and the Walker Brothers, who were just tall fuckers anyhow. We presumed we were going to the television centre studio, but we presumed wrongly. Kustard told us that the show was produced by an outside broadcast unit, who were also his drinking and raving pals at the weekend. They had a very limited budget but creative carte blanche, and the location was always the same, in the basement of a restaurant somewhere in or near the city. Or did we go to another town? Bilzen! Ghent! Knockle! Don't ask me the proper spelling or pronunciation; they all looked the fucking same, and the few faces that we saw in whatever places we were always looked sour.

It started to make sense to me why the paintings of René Magritte—the Belgian Surrealist and Fantasist whose work was popular with the art-school hippie acidheads of the early '60s in London—always had the face covered, blank or incorporated into an objet d'art. His wife committed suicide by jumping off a bridge and drowning in a river near their home . . . She must have fucking hated Belgium too. The drowning, blank, suffocation theme became a disturbing focus in his work from that time on; his ideas were claustrophobic, like the place itself.

"Fucking mind-blowing or what!" . . . Simon

Dupree & the Big Sound were in the bin. What we saw when we entered the basement was each member of the band, five in total, standing up to their waists in shiny corrugated metal rubbish bins, playing their guitars; even the drummer was playing his kit while standing inside one! Surreal indeed, and to make it even more Freaky Frankie, they were miming to the ethereal and heavenly "Kites" as about 30 teeny schoolgirls, some in knee socks, gawked in amazement at the spectacle in front of them—and still no one smiled.

I looked at Alex, and we both fucking cracked up: The trip was beginning, so open the trap door and fly. The three Shulman Brothers of Simon Dupree were as spaced out as we had been a couple of hours before. Derek Shulman told me later that they had come by van on the night ferry from Dover to Ostende and driven straight to the address. As soon as they finished their slot, they were going back to England, where they had a gig that night at the University of Southampton. They were one of the hardest-working bands around at that time, and two years later, when they changed their name to Gentle Giant, they took their work schedule to another level.

As Simon Dupree and also as Gentle Giant, they developed their own unique sound featuring the Mellotron—they were one of the first bands to use it live onstage, and with their own string section (Ray, Derek and Phil Shulman were classically trained and played cello, viola and violin), they could mix the rock with the Baroque . . . "Barock" would be a good way to describe it, I suppose. A talented bunch of fuckers they were. The Ryan twins appeared from somewhere, claiming they were next in line for the production team to let rip on "Eloise," but we stood our ground. Fair play to Kustard; he used his influence with his director pal, and they agreed as we were originally told, that we would go before those cheeky fucking monkees from North London with all their showbiz razzmatazz. They retreated upstairs to the bar, part of which had been commandeered as a makeup and wardrobe area.

The production just seemed to take off around us—it felt as if they were winging it, but we realised later that the team knew exactly what one another were up to. They were full-time employees of the main network, and making this pop TV show was their fun day of the weekly professional schedule. Well, that's what it felt like to us, because they were having a laugh, and that was a new experience for our first visit to Belgium. The bins had been carried away for another day, and a grand piano was wheeled in for Alex, with his mini-moog on top; I stripped off to my underpants, strapped on my angel wings, and with my guitar in the perfect position, we took to the studio floor to do a mime performance of "Pentecost Hotel."

I am glad to say that other than writing about it here, the only other documentary evidence of that hallucinatory event is the photograph reprinted in this book. The Audrey Hepburn (she was from Belgium) teen look-alikes who were in attendance—now either mums, nuns and grannies—took part in this British pop invasion malarky every Friday and watched it the following night on *The Show of the Week* with Mum and Dad. "That's me there, next to the angel with the guitar, Mum!" Dad: "They're all taking drugs, they're as high as a kite!" Daughter: "Angels don't take drugs, they're high enough already." I wondered what they thought! And what about the Singing Nun? She was from Belgium and gave the world "Dominique" to lalala for months on end.

When you abandon your principles, you start to believe that you have the ability to fascinate those around you, and that era was perfect for loose living, loose language, loose morals, and letting other people and situations control the substance of your narrative as you became just another overhyped article for whichever magazine, TV or radio station . . . And indeed, a series of radio and magazine interviews were the next commitment on the Nirvana itinerary.

Kustard left for Amsterdam. I think he'd had enough of our madness, and Promoman and his assistant Veronique took over the reins of the wagon. This time it was a Mercedes 370D, the favourite wheels of Adolf ("Adie Baby") Hitler.

The Walker Brothers (who were not real brothers) had used the car in the morning to do their interviews and had left some gear in the drinks cabinet. We started on that as soon as we were on the road.

I felt wrecked, and Veronique said that she would take me back to the hotel by taxi; Alex would go on with Promo and do the interviews alone. We went to bed for a few hours, and I started to feel much better. I told her, "I fucking hate Belgium," and she said, "I fucking hate it too." In the evening, we had another round of magazine interviews. Alex decided that he felt rough, so Veronique took him back to the hotel. I did our business, and when I got back, he was feeling fully recovered.

Promo told us that we were invited to a "happening" in Antwerp on the Saturday night; it was on the cards that we could have some of the action, because we were not leaving for Germany until the following day. It was taking place in a castle that in the previous century belonged to Peter Benoit, a Flemish classical composer of repute. Now it was the home of Ferre Grignard and 30 of his hippie-commune friends, who partied, painted, and made music and love. Ferre was a folk skiffle singer and had a worldwide hit song called "Ring Ring I've Got To Sing." I had never heard of it or him, but Alex, who was living in Paris in 1965, was aware of his success and the eccentric bohemian lifestyle he and his crowd led, as they were constantly in the news for scandals of some sort or other. Promoman told us, "Think outrageous with a capital 'O'—that's what it's going to be like"; he had been before. Now we were talking business; maybe there was a Belgian or at least an Antwerp scene after all, and Ferre might come up with the fucking goods.

We were fully paid-up members of the Slumberland Club for most of the following day, and in the evening watched the Simon Dupree and Nirvana slots of the TV show, which, much to our amazement, were impressive . . . and it worked. The production people had tightened up all the shots and intercut newsreel footage with graphic effects. The pop-music films were then slotted into the live variety show of local well-known singing, comedy and dancing acts, but it was fucking endless, and we never saw the Ryans or the Walkers—we were going to a "happening."

Promo picked us up from the hotel, and we were on the coast before our makeup was dry. There was just one entrance, a great oak-panelled double gate. Promo spoke to someone through a small hatch that was drawn across, and whatever he said worked; the gate parted, and we were in the courtyard of the cars. There must have been at least 200 guests milling around—some in full flowing regalia, some in cloaks or capes (they were fashionable at the time for men and women), others in fancy dress, and some in no dress—just masks, thongs and boots. "I should have brought my fucking wings,"

I said. "I don't think we 're going to need wings to be fucking flying here, man," Alex summed up the moment to perfection.

Angels walk with halos, devils with horns, a canvas with arrows, couples in coffins, a harp with no strings, a box full of bluebells, a fly with no wings, incense and icons, hash bamboo shuffle, a chocolate iguana, a jar full of truffle . . . and this was only the hall of introduction. *"Head" girls from Hamburg, outcasts in drag, circles of queens, an American flag . . .* then I met Fabien, who told me it was not a "happening" but a subversive plot to overthrow Peter Pan, who was Ferre's alter ego. I met three different guys who said they were Ferre Grignard, I don't even know if the real Ferre was there. Alex told me later that he was, but Promo confused the issue even more when he told us that Ferre used doubles. One of the Ferres I met was playing guitar and singing, "I'm an anarchist, I'm a singer, I'm a bohemian and a beggar"; he should have said, "I'm a fucking ringer!" This was where the Festival of Venus became Sodom and Gomorrah, where a big bollocks with no brain started grunting and growling our name into our faces, "Nirvana! Nirvana!" He must have fucking hated the TV show, as much as he hated himself and fucking Belgium.

When Alex and I went somewhere to party or hang out and get into some action, we always went our separate ways and did our own thing, as we did not want to be perceived as being gay, which sometimes happened. We were in each other's pockets for two years by that time, and being together so much, you became as one. I did not see Alex again until we left the castle sometime in the early morning with Promo hustling us out unexpectedly.

The "happening" or the "Peter Pan Plot," as Fabien described it, was on three floors. The ground level had food, drink and silver plates with readymade spliffs, quality help-yourself, I was told by Tante from the port of Antwerp. There was a large banqueting table laid out with an assortment of cold meats, cheeses of every description, salmon, caviar and paté of the region, and a lamb and a suckling pig were roasting on a double spit . . . It was in every sense of the word a Feast . . . Le Grand Boeuf!

On the floor above was a dancing *get out of your box* trip-and-crash space where some were already *in the box* (lying in coffinlike bunkbeds that had stereo speakers inside). The second floor was a number of rooms with slide projection images on the walls and mattresses on the floor where naked couples and groups moved felinely in the liquid purple lights.

We had a golden rule when we went to party in a risk atmosphere such as this "happening": Drink only what you poured, and smoke only what you made yourself. I had been spiked once before under dubious circumstances at the home of a well-known songwriter in London W12, and that twisted-lightning experience was not something I wanted to relive. I popped a bottle of the best champagne I could find and settled down to observe the shenanigans.

I was wrestling with angels when Promo started to pull me out of there. "Alex is already in the car," he said. Promo had a tip-off from someone he knew in the police force that the place was going to be raided, and he should get out of there and take whoever was with him right away.

Promo told us that there had been talk of a black-magic ritual, maybe even cannibalism, and suspicion surrounding the disappearance of a young hippie who had been staying at the castle. There had been previous raids by the police, but no one was ever charged with an offence.

Promo added that Ferre often received 10,000 francs for a show but would be broke a few days later; it was expensive keeping a family of thirsty sponges in party mode. But that's how he was—he would prefer to drink and smoke it rather than give it to the tax man. "Ferre must have fucking hated Belgium too," was our unified response.

I was never dependent on drugs or on drink; I dropped acid a few times, and it was nothing to write home about. But when I took speed, that was another trip altogether, and I swore a lot, as Alex did when he took whiskey. I have tried here to capture in the writing the way it really was for us on our first tour in Belgium. We were doing speed and whiskey, and our behaviour was obnoxious, especially our lingo and the use of the word "fuck" in communicating with each other and those we met. It came with the territory of our business and travels in music, but Belgium was a place that really fucked us off.

If "fuck" is a serious swear word, then we and everybody we met in studios, record companies and on the road swore seriously and often. In Ireland, it was "feck" or "feckin" (think Father Ted and Father Jack); in England it was "fuck" or "fucking." I was at home with either, and I could always switch off if I was in different or more polite surroundings; then I would revert to the lingo of reckless swearing as soon as I was back with the rock reprobates, and if I took speed I was often over the top. We were self-indulgent, immoral and without principles sometimes, like barbarians; as much as we were creative, calm and sharing with our music, we could be destructive and irresponsible in hurting those who were closest to us. I met others from different bands who had the same confession in their eyes, and the symptomatic behaviour was always recognizable, though we rarely confided in one another.

Just as some people and places can be comfortable and calming, other people and places can be disturbing . . . That's why I fucking hated Belgium.

If I go there today, I still feel a kind of alienation, but that is probably my subconscious thoughts from 40 years ago prodding me. Belgium is a different place, and I am a different person, thank God; a lot has changed for the better in that time, as it has in Alex's Greece and the Ireland of my youth.

Indulgent Recommendation for the iPod Generation

Simon Dupree & the Big Sound, *Part of My Past* (anthology, EMI)

Count Five, *Psychotic Reaction* (1965)

The Nashville Teens, *Tobacco Road* (1964)

The Yardbirds, *Good Morning Little Schoolgirl* (1964)

THE SALVADOR DALI SHOW
1968-69

A number of things made Nirvana of the psychedelic '60s a unique group. For a start, we brought together the elements of classical and jazz, blues and rock, lyrical and "beat" language. Then there was the unusual combination of a Greek and an Irishman; our diverse cultural backgrounds encouraged our natural curiosity about our surroundings in the metropolis that was London, our new adopted home away from home . . . .

In 1968, we were the first group to have an album, *The Story of Simon Simopath,* released on Island Records, the first and most important British independent; today it's called Island/Universal. (John Martyn's solo LP London Conversations launched the label.) We were the first group to introduce an electric cello as part of our live gigs and in the studio. (A band from the West Coast of America Alex liked called *It's a Beautiful Day* were using an electric violin, and Arthur Lee and Bryan MacLean with the group *Love*, also from the West Coast USA, were making the groundbreaking *Forever Changes*, one of the classic albums of all time, which would feature sublime strings arranged by David Angel.) We were one of the first few groups—the others were the Small Faces and the Beatles—to use phasing, a studio technique that produces a jet-type sound, the sonic result of two blended sounds with cyclical wave frequencies.

And we are the only rock group in the world to have performed live on television with Salvador Dali, the Spanish Catalan Surrealist painter . . . "Now that is unique," as Dali would say in his elongated French "Englese" pronunciation—"*incrediblé*!" When Dali spoke, by way of performance, he could make some words last 20 seconds or longer; what a fucking mad genius he was.

The first time I became aware of Salvador Dali was in 1963, when I borrowed a book about Paris' Dada movement from the library at Ealing Art College. It had three of his paintings in it, including the still life *Basket of Bread*—you wanted to eat the bread off the page, it was so fucking real. The others were *The Angelus at Milet* and *The Crucifixion of Christ,* both truly brilliant and masterful paintings, the work of a meticulous craftsman. What struck me instantly about the paintings was that they created a space where you could dream. The more I examined his work and read about him, the more I realised that he was up there with the most well-known artists such as Picasso and Chagall. I discovered his Soft Watch Melting and Soft Clock Exploding, and the three paintings he did of Gala, his wife and muse, collectively known as The Madonna of Port Lligat.

Gala loved money, luxury and Dali, but she liked young men also. Dali was a voyeur; their marriage was never consummated, but he loved her. I discovered *Hallucinogenic Toreador, Enigma of Hitler, Autumn Cannibalism, Swans Reflecting Elephants, Lobster Telephone, Leda Atomica, Woman With the Head of Flowers* . . . I was hooked like so many others I have met over the years, and I decided to visit Dali's holiday resort of Cadaques, north of Barcelona, on a short trip via the Magic Bus.

Born in 1904, Dali lived in his paternal home in Figueres until his father disowned and disinherited him in 1930 because of his involvement with Gala and with the Surrealists Breton, Miró, Paul Eluard (who was the former husband of Gala) and the other political animals of the Parisian scene. Dali also refused to apologise publicly for a provocative statement, "Sometimes I spit for fun on my mother's portrait," with which he captioned a drawing titled *The Sacred Heart of Jesus Christ* in a Paris exhibition; the father-son relationship ceased to exist. Dali, as a departing present, handed his father a condom with his own sperm inside, saying, "Take that. Now I owe you nothing"—a typical Dada act. Dali's mother had died when he was 16, and his brother died at 3 the year before he was born.

Dali and Gala rented a small fisherman's cottage at Port Lligat, a short walk around the bay from Cadaques. They eventually bought it, and over the next 30 years enlarged it to become Casa Dali, a fantasy studio and villa, and a unique Surrealistic architectural achievement.

Starting in 1931 with one of his most well-known paintings, *The Persistence of Memory* (sometimes called

Soft Watches), over the next three decades Dali produced a breathtaking body of work in painting, sculpture, jewellery, design, film production and writing. In his own words, "I am painting pictures that make me die for joy, that inspire me with profound emotion." Making extensive use of symbolism in his work, he painted *Metamorphosis of Narcissus, The Burning Giraffe, Sublime Moment, The Temptation of Saint Anthony, Young Virgin Auto-Sodomized by the Horns of Her Own Chastity* and *Honey Is Sweeter Than Blood,* and he reworked *The Great Masturbator* from two years before. Dali's genius, though flawed, was recognised worldwide. He worked on stage designs for Garcia Lorca theatre productions in Madrid and Barcelona, and in film for the Marx Brothers, for Walt Disney (an animated film called *Destino*, completed by Roy Disney in 2003) and for Jack Warner Studios in Hollywood (Dali is responsible for the dream sequence in Alfred Hitchcock's *Spellbound*). He did book illustrations, lithographs and posters, and painted portraits of Laurence Olivier (as Richard III), Mae West (portrait and Lips sofa design), and Wallis Simpson and her husband, the Duke of Windsor.

Dali had an ambivalent attitude toward money,

whereas Gala adored dollars, so he worked to satisfy her needs. He did understand that to become world-famous, you had to know wealthy and influential people, and possess a talent for self-publicity, which he had in plentiful and original ways.

Dali and Gala moved to New York for eight years as the Second World War started in Europe, and in 1949 returned to Port Lligat. A lapsed Catholic who returned with fervent devotion in the later years of his life, Dali was fascinated with religions; he was into mysticism, Christian iconography, optical illusions, geometry, nuclear physics, masturbation and voyeurism. Though his decadent behaviour and eccentric manner became more important to him than his art, Gala, a Russian immigrant, made sure that his paintings were changing hands at high prices. By the 1960s, the two were spending their summers in Cadaques (Port Lligat) and winters in New York—Gala loved the cold and the snow.

I was drawn irretrievably to Dali's luxuriant talent the way a pilgrim is drawn to a sacred or miraculous place. I felt an affinity between the psychedelic, trippy, ethereal, spacy world of London, where my music was, and the paradoxical statements and hidden dreams of Dali's seascape at Port Lligat on the Mediterranean coast. Some of Nirvana's followers and some journalists have speculated whether the Nirvana song "Pentecost Hotel" was written under the influence of drugs, LSD specifically. No—but it was written under the influence of Dali. The song was the nearest I could get to achieving what a fantasist/Surrealist painter could achieve on a naked canvas.

There underneath blue waves, the sunlight spreads blue rays
and Pentecost Hotel shades all its cobwebs.
Explosion of the stars upon the sea in red
and all the guests that see the water fireworks.
And in the lobby Magdalena is friendly to all the people with a passport of insanity, and seven sirens
are a-dancing to music in Pentecost Hotel.
Strange viaduct of beams, take me to all your dreams
And leave me there as master of the ocean.
There underneath blue waves the sunshine spreads blue rays
And Pentecost Hotel shades all its cobwebs.

--"Pentecost Hotel"

With a 10-pound open return ticket on the Magic Bus out of Victoria Coach Station in London, in 1969 I embarked on a 40-hour journey—cross-channel ferry boat, then down across France to Perpignan, Port Bou over the frontier to Spain, and on to Barcelona, where I backtracked the short train ride to Figueres and then hitched a ride out to Cadaques. I walked over to Port Lligat the next morning to find that I was one of about 20 Dali acolytes and travellers all hoping to catch a glimpse of the Genius.

The studio where Dali painted was much too high above the level of the beach to be able to see inside the panorama window that faced the ocean, but you could spend days in endless fixation looking at the house. Cadaques was the summer playground for the Barcelona set, but it had also become a hedonistic hangout for poets, writers, painters, hippies and druggies—the La Movida of the beautiful people. If London was swinging, I can tell you Cadaques was fucking flying; everything was for free, including love, and the laid-back action was around the clock, the midnight beach party being the highlight of every day. I went out to Port Lligat each afternoon, and the same people were there—Germans,

Americans, Aussies, Dutch, Japanese . . . If a curtain moved on any of the windows, especially the studio, someone would rush about shouting, "I saw him! I saw him! Look over there!" Some of the fishermen and their wives who lived in the cottages opposite the Dali house went in by a side porch through a small wooden door with a religious motif on it; they had their own key, so I assumed they were staff. They would never answer our questions about Dali—all sworn to silence by Gala, I found out later. There was no front or main entrance to the house; it was high stone walls on three sides, the ocean on the other.

The upper roof level was adorned by two gigantic Perspex eggs that were lit from the inside at night and visible to passing ships far out at sea; inside the walls of the terraced gardens stood a life-size model of a giraffe that was moved by someone to different positions during the day—many were fooled into believing that it was the real thing . . . maybe Dali was at home? At Port Lligat, it was mind-blowing to observe the changing light—the sunsets and sunrises, the rock formations in amongst the lapping and breaking waves. Moving shadows shaped faces on the landscape; the breeze and the wind played rhythms on shifting sand dunes, illusion and fantasy dancing at midnight. It was an inspirational place, and the 40 hours it had taken me to get there melted like a Dali "soft watch" in the pleasures of those moments.

Towards the end of the week, I was at the Central bar in Cadaques and met Captain Peter Moore and his Swiss-French wife, Catherine. Peter, who was born in Ireland and brought up in France, told me he had been Dali's private secretary since 1962. He had worked in the film industry and was introduced to Dali by the producer Alexander Korda during the making of the 1945 film *Richard III*. He said to forget about seeing Dali at the house, as the artist and Gala had been in Paris for the past month and would not be back until early September. So much for the moving curtains and the shifting giraffe; the house staff, the fishermen and their families accounted for all that, Peter told me with a smile. Peter and Catherine invited me to their home in Cadaques, to show me some private Dali works they were collecting for a new gallery they were planning to open the following year. We got on like a giraffe on fire, and I was invited back whenever I could make it. After spending some time with them, I felt that there was an inner sanctum of Dali associates in Cadaques, and Captain Moore was as close as I was going to get to it for now. I left Cadaques the next day for the return ride to London on the Magic Bus. It had been a week of wine and waves, sleepless nights and El Dorado days; now it was time to make some music, and we did.

Imagine my sublime moment in July 1968, two years later, when Island Records' promotion department told us that Nirvana had been invited to appear on a television show in Paris with Salvador Dali; the show was called *Improvisation on a Sunday Afternoon (L'improvisation sur un après-midi Dimanche)*. It was for the main French channel, TV1, and our fee was very generous. I was completely fazed, as were Alex and the rest of the band. Penny Hanson, our liaison at Island for TV promotion, told us that we were to arrive at the studio in Paris for midday, set up our equipment (it was a live show), have three songs ready to perform on cue (including "Rainbow Chaser," which had just been released in France) and, last but not least, to look and sound as psychedelic as possible. We were on a high for days, and somewhere in that high the thought crossed my mind that maybe Captain Moore had something to do with this most unusual booking; he was, after all, responsible for marketing Dali abroad, and he knew everybody in the film and TV world in England and France. I remembered he had said to me that the film world was no different from the art world; they were both run by Jewish businessmen. Fate works in mysterious ways, and we were both in the Celtic brotherhood, so maybe that helped.

On the Sunday we arrived in Paris, we were totally smashed, tripping in our own psychedelic atmospherics. All I remember was being in London at the Portobello Road market in Notting Hill on the Saturday morning; after that I have no idea what happened until I was sitting by the Seine in Paris 24 hours later . . . But that afternoon's performance TV show I will remember forever.

The network TV schedule was open-ended, which meant the programme might last an hour or much longer, depending on the mood and creative whims of its central guest. It was produced once a month, and the previous month's guest had been Sophia Loren.

The concept was a live performance and interview

improvisation with Dali, who would be free to roam around the floor space in an environment of specially prepared props that would tease his imagination and commentary. Nirvana was the live music, and following Dali's every wild improvised move and taking in his every blasphemous word were an invited "Who's Who" from Paris café society plus models, dancers, students, actors, some drummers from North Africa, a couple of bebop saxophone players, the presenter and two freewheeling hoist cameras on trolleys. The scene was set, and we were in the eye of the storm, being the only static force in Dali's working space. We had one rehearsal for a sound balance, and another for the cameramen and producers with the audience in the room, and they fucking loved us; they were as out of it as we were. I think everyone was off his trolley that day, including the cameramen and the presenter. The French can be fucking brilliantly crazy sometimes as much as they can be fucking boringly blasé a lot of the time.

The programme went out live to the public at 3 p.m., but Dali had not yet arrived, so the presenter started to whip up the atmosphere in the room. As the cameras panned around above at a ferociously dangerous speed, our drummer nearly lost his head standing up to smash the cymbals on his drum kit. The atmosphere was electric, and I could feel that we were about to be part of a historic Dali "happening."

There was a hushed silence for a minute, and then the buzz started. It became tribal when the drummers and saxophones let rip with beats and screams; the crowd and the presenter were shouting "Dali! Dali! Dali!" Then, floating in stage smoke and incense, the guest of honour came through the white paper wall that hung in rolls all over the large studio. On a dual lead, Dali was holding two young Bengali tigers—either tame or drugged, but their colouring was spectacular. On either side of him was a blonde Lolita, topless, in glitter hot pants in Stars & Stripes material and cowboy boots. They were no more than "sweet little 16"; Alex was convinced they were transvestites. They proceeded to remove Dali's magenta-and-gold cloak and throw it out in front of him; he went down on his knees to kiss the ground, then shouted over and over, "Dali el Papa, Dali el Papa," and started to give everyone in the room his blessings while some of the crowd kissed the diamonds and rubies that were on his hands . . . It was all "happening." I could see that Dali had taken in the room, everything in it and every person, in a couple of craning birdlike twists of his neck; he was as sharp as a razor, as fast as a gunslinger. Space Ship Dali had landed!

I can only guess the reaction of the French Sunday-afternoon TV audience to this madness; it was either indifference (because all of France knew of Dali's crazy antics and publicity stunts), or it was a shock-horror show.

Dali was dressed in a scarlet velvet suit with a white silk shirt of the Regency style and green leather riding boots; his long silver hair and the famous upturned moustache were groomed to perfection. The show that went out on television was two hours of mesmerising exhibitionism. Dali worked at a phenomenal speed, then suddenly he would stop, stand still, stare at the camera and declare in elongated sentences, "Dali is the greatest, the best, the most popular and talented person in the world! Dali needs no *sedativo*, only sex with boys!" Then off he went to the next prop.

Dali had his own invented language, and if you

spoke French, English, Spanish or Arabic, you could still understand him because of the way he mixed nouns and verbs from all the languages. The producers had hung four large black-and-white Andy Warhol prints of Chairman Mao, John F. Kennedy, Marilyn Monroe and Che Guevara on the partitioned white walls. There was a large wooden cross with a life-size model of Jesus nailed to it; it was covered in purple cloth, as they do with statues and crucifixes during Lent (the 40 days before Easter the Catholic Church devotes to fasting and repentance). At the base of the cross was a golden stepladder. A large antique oak table with Dali Signature boxes full of the most expensive chocolate sweets Paris could produce for the occasion stood in one corner; a larger-than-life-size bronze sculpture of *Picador on a Horse* by Picasso stood in another corner; there were dozens of Venetian cut-glass jars filled with paints of every conceivable colour, and next to them, ivory-handled paintbrushes of every size. Nirvana was in the other corner waiting for the producers' cue to play our first song, "Rainbow Chaser."

Dali had climbed the ladder at the foot of the cross and cut open the cloth with a scissors to reveal the face and body of Jesus; he then force-fed chocolate sweets from a box into Jesus' mouth, all the time making commentary in his lingo—his manifesto, he called it. The producer gave us our cue, and we started to play "Rainbow Chaser," at which point Dali scrambled back down the ladder, rushing towards the music, and blessed us with electric blue paint from one of the jars on the floor, spattering our clothes and, most seriously, the cello, which was old and valuable. We kept playing; there was no other choice—it was a live, recorded "happening."

The eventual outcome was a letter that Muff Winwood showed me on our return to England, claiming compensation from the French television company "for cleaning and restoring the cello professionally." When you are in the moment of something like that, it does not occur to you to ask Dali after the show to sign a shirt, a jacket, even the cello; it would be worth a massive amount of money today. He would have refused, I am sure; he knew how much his signature was worth. It was a moot point, as afterward Dali was nowhere to be seen, gone as he had come, in a cloud of incense and smoke . . . back to Planet Dali.

Everything was happening fast for us at that time, and it was difficult to believe that we were there playing with the world's most famous living painter. But the musical reality of the event was confirmed a few weeks later when Françoise Hardy, the legendary French pop queen, called our publisher in Paris to say that she was going to record "Tiny Goddess" in three languages—French, English and German; she had seen and heard us perform the song on the show. So it did "happen," after all.

Indulgent Recommendation for the iPod Generation

Salvador Dali was passionate about only one piece of music:

Richard Wagner's opera "Tristan and Isolde." Check it out sometime . . . it's a trip!

CHRIS BLACKWELL

The late and great Frank Zappa said, "Music is a decoration to fragments of time . . . without time nothing can happen, without music to decorate it, time is a bunch of boring production lines, or a collection of dates by which bills must be paid."

I can identify with that perception of music, word for word. I cannot imagine a day without some music—making it, listening to it, thinking about it. Music is with me consciously and subconsciously, and if you are a creator at work in music, painting, sculpture, dance, theatre, poetry or writing, you will know and understand where I am coming from.

Though Chris is different, he is far from a

stereotypical music businessman. He is not a musician; I doubt if he can even sing or whistle a tune. But he has the right feeling to communicate in the musicians' domain, where his combined talent, knowledge and production ideas are second to none. On top of that, with his business ability to find ideas with potential for global success, he is truly a one-off.

Over the four years we were signed to Island Records, the pink label took on a life of its own, and many of the staff when speaking about Chris would use his initials—C.B., or just "Blackwell." Maybe it was not that important, but it made me uncomfortable, and I could not explain why. I was working with him, not for him, and when he addressed me as "Patrick" at our first meeting, I naturally called him Chris from there on, and continued to do so, as on the occasion when Alex and I were invited to the Island 25th Anniversary Party in 1984, and in 1999, when I encountered him in Manchester, where he was a guest speaker on the panel at the "In the City" music forum.

Before I signed with Chris, I had read or heard . . . that he was a white Jamaican, whatever that was supposed to mean . . . that his father was Irish and his mother from an aristocratic background, but he had been disinherited . . . that he was part of the Crosse and Blackwell family . . . that he was handsome, and women followed him around . . . that he had been to public school in England . . . that he was in property and tourism . . . that he used to rent scooters at the beach at Ocho Rios . . . that he liked to gamble in the casinos . . . that he imported blue-beat and ska records and sold them from a mini-van around the specialist shops in London . . . that he discovered Millie Small and the song "My Boy Lollipop," which became a massive hit on the Phillips label . . . and that he started Island Records on a bank loan of £2,000.

Wow! If you painted that composite onto a blank canvas, it would be a very spirited painting indeed. I liked the gambling reference, because I always thought he would be a very good poker player, but really, I was not that interested in his background or upbringing. Alex and I were both too busy in the moment, getting to know him and the way he worked in the everyday present.

Chris' focus and enthusiasm were infectious, and during our four years on the Island pink label (the pink

Island Records Limited
Directors: Christopher Blackwell, David Betteridge, Christopher Peers
155/157 Oxford Street, London, W.1
Cable Address: ACKEE Telephone: Reg 6228

8th July 1969.

Messrs. P. Campbell-Lyons &
A. Spyropoulos,
13 Creffield Road,
London W. 5.

Re: NIRVANA - Reg. No.JH1318224

Dear Pat and Alex:

We confirm that we have relinquished all our rights to the business name 'NIRVANA', which is now owned by both of you.

Yours sincerely,
ISLAND RECORDS LTD.

Christopher Blackwell
Managing Director.

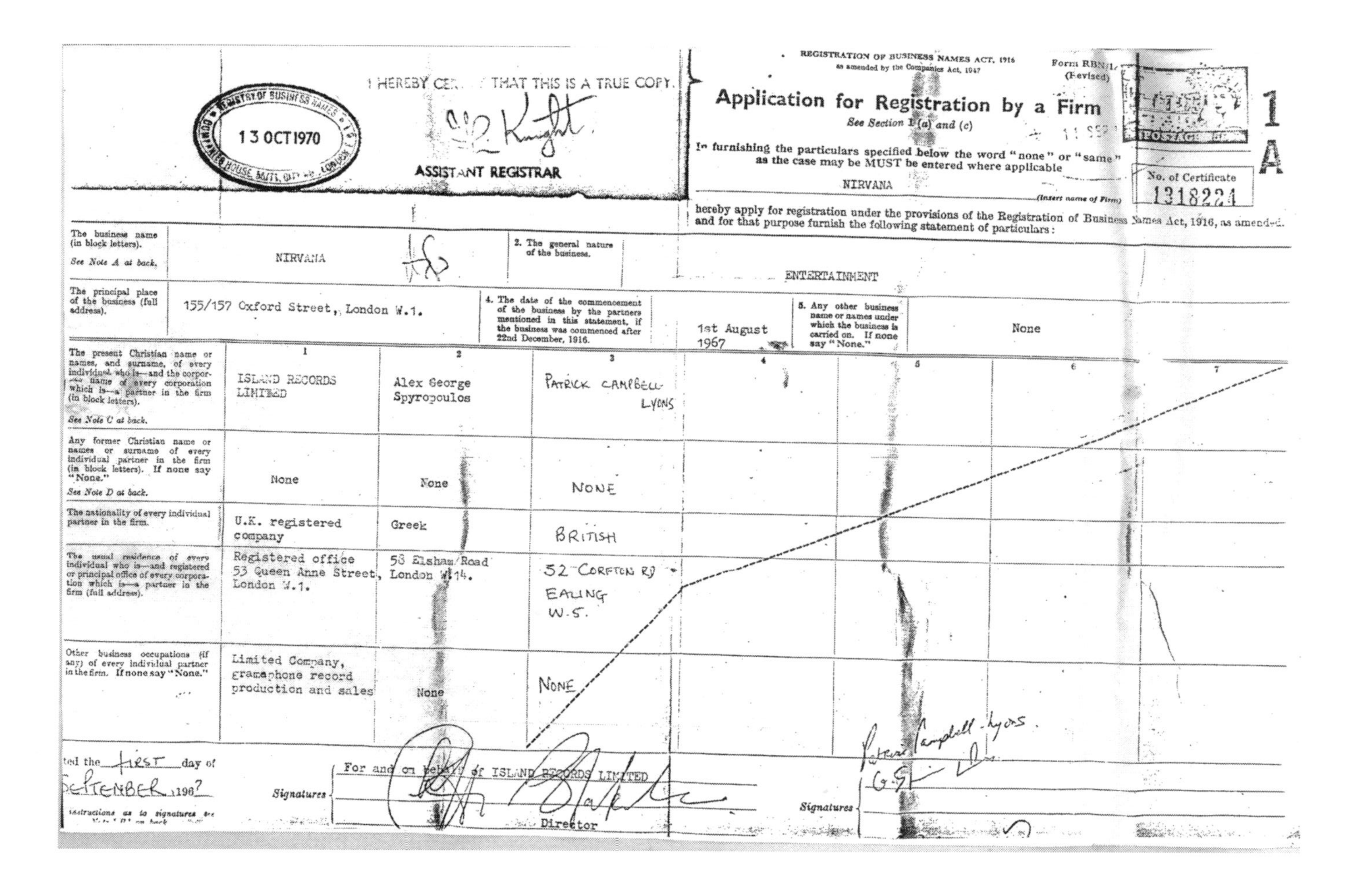

REGISTRATION OF BUSINESS NAMES ACT, 1916
as amended by the Companies Act, 1947

Form RBN/1 (Revised)

1A

Application for Registration by a Firm

See Section 1 (a) and (c)

In furnishing the particulars specified below the word "none" or "same" as the case may be MUST be entered where applicable

No. of Certificate 1318224

NIRVANA *(Insert name of Firm)*

hereby apply for registration under the provisions of the Registration of Business Names Act, 1916, as amended and for that purpose furnish the following statement of particulars:

The business name (in block letters). *See Note A at back.*	NIRVANA	2. The general nature of the business.	ENTERTAINMENT
The principal place of the business (full address).	155/157 Oxford Street, London W.1.	4. The date of the commencement of the business by the partners mentioned in this statement, if the business was commenced after 22nd December, 1916.	1st August 1967
5. Any other business name or names under which the business is carried on. If none say "None."	None		

	1	2	3	4	5	6	7
The present Christian name or names, and surname, of every individual who is—and the corporate name of every corporation which is—a partner in the firm (in block letters). *See Note C at back.*	ISLAND RECORDS LIMITED	Alex George Spyropoulos	PATRICK CAMPBELL-LYONS				
Any former Christian name or names or surname of every individual partner in the firm (in block letters). If none say "None." *See Note D at back.*	None	None	NONE				
The nationality of every individual partner in the firm.	U.K. registered company	Greek	BRITISH				
The usual residence of every individual who is—and registered or principal office of every corporation which is—a partner in the firm (full address).	Registered office 53 Queen Anne Street, London W.1.	58 Elsham Road London W.14.	52 CORFTON RD EALING W.5.				
Other business occupations (if any) of every individual partner in the firm. If none say "None."	Limited Company, gramaphone record production and sales	None	NONE				

Dated the FIRST day of SEPTEMBER 1967

Signatures: For and on behalf of ISLAND RECORDS LIMITED [signature] Director

Signatures: Patrick Campbell-Lyons [signature]

Instructions as to signatures are ... on back

I always see as the Island years; for me after 'pink' it was just another record company), he created a free, open-door atmosphere at the Oxford Street building. Chris was there and always accessible to the musicians, producers and songwriters who came in on a regular basis and used it as a second creative home. It felt like being in a brand-new country that was being governed by the people, and Chris was our elected president.

Interestingly, Jamaica achieved its independence in 1962, the year Chris left for England to pursue his dream. Our paths may have even crossed then, because I used to go to the Shepherds Bush market to buy blue-beat records, and he was selling them with his partner, Dave Betteridge, to the stall holders. It's all about those ley lines and bloodlines, about the attitude and aptitude of those around you in your formative years. As an Irishman knowing my ancestral and historical lineage, I can say it's also about slavery, oppression and indoctrination, about the freedom to have an education and practise one's beliefs; it's about the ability to rise above the normal acceptance of things; it's about courage and strength. It's your place, it's your country, it's your roots, and it's your soul.

Chris understood those things. He was wise beyond his years, and at the time I was not; I was still searching, learning, and yearning for new adventures. But it did not take too long, as I had the advantage of being taught history and geography when I was at school, growing up in the Republic of Ireland, by a very wise and brilliant teacher.

Chris is only six years older than me; he was 29 in 1967, when we signed with him—of an age to have been in our group, but for me, he was a taller figure that I looked up to, as much as our music mentor and friend. And those four years, signed to the best British label ever, were the most secure that I have felt in the music business, and the most creatively rewarding. Nirvana's profile today, 40 years later, remains as strong as it ever was; our recordings have stood the test of time and get played regularly. A big part of that is down to Chris giving us the support and creative freedom we needed to achieve something with substance.

It was normal routine, when we were in London, for Alex Spyropoulos and I to turn up at the office and use the music room when it was free, playing our demos to Chris and producer Jimmy Miller. Muff Winwood might give an opinion; Chris Peers, the promotion man, would tell us if it had a chance to get airplay, and Elsa would type out lyrics and make endless cups of coffee. Various members and roadies of Traffic, Spooky Tooth, Free, the Smoke (I never really knew what was going on with them—were they signed?), Jimmy Cliff and Jackie Edwards (a wonderful man and a talented writer) were there like us, doing their thing, as were John and Beverly Martyn, newly arrived on the scene.

Lionel Conway, the publisher, was about to leave Dick James Music and set up Blue Mountain Music for Chris. Elton John and Bernie Taupin, two of Conway's writers, were also rumoured to be joining him. Lionel made the move, while Elton and Bernie, even though they were playing new songs in the Island office and seemed to all intents and purposes to be a part of the scene, never made that final contractual obligation; I often wonder why.

Joe Cocker from Sheffield, his keyboard man Chris Stainton, and Tony Visconti, a new blow-in from New York who arranged strings and played cello and flute, were involved with Denny Cordell, whose office was on the opposite side of the street, but they used the Island music rooms for playbacks and to do routine backing vocals with Sue and Sunny Wheatman, the best in the business. Sue and Sunny were the partners of John Glover and Alec Leslie, who were doing agency and management with Island, as Chris wanted the bands out on the road as soon as possible. I heard at least ten different mixes of Cocker's cover of the Beatles' "With a Little Help From My Friends" during the weeks Cordell was trying to get it spot-on, finding the right balance between Joe's sublime vocal and the soul sisters Sue and Sunny. The song title really does describe the working atmosphere of the early Island pink days at Oxford Street. Denny would play those mixes to everyone, to get a feel or a suggestion that might improve the track. He was so close to it all the time, but he persisted and got it right. It is the perfect single, a pop classic; it became Joe Cocker's calling card to the world.

As far as Nirvana was concerned, Chris convinced us that we were the best in our style of music. We were his golden boys for a while, but that was part of his talent; he was able to make all his artists feel they were special. Muff Winwood said to Alex and me, "Blackwell signed you because Procol Harum turned him down."

Well, that may be so, but I never felt we were a substitute for them. I knew Chris was risking everything on his own intuition, and that made it all the more exciting. I think Muff got it wrong, and it was Chris that turned down Procol Harum . . . but that's another story, like Muff's bass line on "Gimme Some Lovin'."

To this day, people ask me what it was like to be in at the beginning of Island, a label now spoken of as legendary. My answer is always the same: Listen to the music . . . it will tell you everything.

Elektra Records in the USA was the other label we would have liked to have been on—that would have been the perfect place for our music over there, but it did not happen. Our first album was released in America on Bell Records. Nobody knew about it, not even us; it disappeared into the Garden of Rapid Delights.

So who is the enigmatic Chris Blackwell?

I never saw him wear a tie; I don't believe he owns one. I never heard him swear, use foul language or badmouth anyone. His word is always his bond; he finds it easy to forgive. I never saw him smoke or take drugs. He likes women, and they like him. He is a Gemini. He is never happy about doing interviews or self-publicity. He can be shy at times; he says little about his past, whether successes, failures or setbacks, and his personal life is private (until the day he may decide to write his autobiography!). He has a good humorous turn off phrase; he has his own indefinable style. But most of all, he enjoys and loves to support original music. He feels it when it is from the heart, and understands where it comes from in others.

Chris has been described as a maverick . . . Sorry! He might be unorthodox at times, but he surely is not undisciplined. He was the founder of the first independent record label, the template for others to follow, and follow they did, all of them a pale imitation of the real thing, and some of them set up by hustlers who could not spell the word vision, never mind have one. He is clever and he is connected, and when I use that word I don't mean he knows the right people in the right places (he probably does!), I mean he is connected to his roots and to others around the world who know what being connected feels like.

A house is made of stone and beams

A home is made of love and dreams

. . . and Chris put his heart and soul and money into making the Island dream a reality. There were no poseurs, rogues, charlatans or puppets around, just young, talented, adventurous and sometimes crazy people, with no agenda other than to make the best music they could, without any fear of failure, and have a ball doing it.

The Irish philosopher priest Fr. John Donohue wrote a wonderful book in the 1980s titled *Anam Cara*, which in the Gaelic language of my country means "soul friend." When I take that book in my hands, it has what I can only describe as a personal radiant glow around it; the beginning of Island had that same kind of glow. Every day was a new journey, and everyone was going in the right direction, for the right reasons.

By the time Island moved to the Basing Street address in Notting Hill, the glow had lost some of its radiance. Alec Waugh published his novel *Island in the Sun in 1955, and in 1957 Harry Belafonte sang Island in the Sun*, a worldwide calypso hit . . . Were they predecessors of the Jamaican glow that Chris brought to his Island in the sun at its beginnings in London town?

I call to mind two personal moments, one from

the beginning and the other towards the end of our time on Island.

I was walking down Oxford Street in London late on a Sunday night in 1968. I had been to the 100 Club to see a band called Warm Sounds. As I approached the junction of Poland Street on the opposite side, I saw the beat-up Mustang that belonged to Chris parked on the corner. I looked up to the Island office floor; the lights were on, and I could clearly see Chris, his back to the window, sitting in Neville the accountant's chair. There are not many people who visit their office to work that late on a Sunday night, and in that moment I realised that Chris' energy and time were focused on the business and financial aspects as much as the creative. It was not an anomaly, either, because the next day when I went there, I shared my observation with Neville, who told me that on Monday mornings when he arrived, he regularly found Chris had left work waiting on his desk.

The second moment occurred on the day Chris released Nirvana from our contract. He felt our third Nirvana LP, *Black Flower, was too orchestral, and he did not want to release it on Island. We met at his home in Fillimore Gardens in Kensington and had a very amicable meeting on the subject. Chris was right; it was very orchestral. He compared it to the soundtrack of the French film A Man and a Woman*, which I took as a compliment at the time—Alex and I thought it was our best album of the three we recorded for Island, and I still think so today. Painful as it was, we agreed to go our own way, and Chris gave us the album to place with another label when we would sign a new deal with whoever.

His parting words were, "If you ever need my help for anything, or there is something I can do for either of you, my door is always open." I know that he meant what he said, and today, 40 years later, I could take up his offer without fear of rejection . . . just like family! The only problem would be finding the right door: Would it be New York, Los Angeles, Miami, London, Dublin, Jamaica, Barbados, Bermuda, Johannesburg, Kenya, Paris? I think my best option now would be to go to the Internet, the window to the world and everybody in it, including Chris.

And I just remembered one more thing! Chris is the only man I know who looked good in sandals. And he wore them all the time, maybe still does.

I met with Chris again in 2008; I had not seen him since the mid-'80s. He was visiting Trinity College in Dublin, which is a distinguished seat of learning, to receive a cultural award medal, an honour not given away lightly as so many of today's awards are. He was in fine form, bright as a lark on a clear morning, connecting with his roots—his father was an Irish merchant who traded with the Caribbean in the '30s.

And now here was Chris, being honoured for his creative contribution to the music of the world, having signed and helped U2 in partnership with Paul McGuinness to become Ireland's greatest export of modern times.

Chris is a smart person, and from the off has always gone with his gut instinct in music and business. He has given so many artists a home where they could express themselves creatively and spiritually, and where in the process they would evolve or occasionally dissolve! And he continues today. Chris sometimes comes across as an outsider to those who don't really know him, but if you are on the inside of his global family of artists and businesspeople, friends and fighters, free spirits and romantics, you realise that he is a true ambassador of music and a man of his word.

I respect and admire him, and it is a great privilege to be a friend.

Indulgent Recommendation for the iPod Generation

Traffic, "No Place, No Name, No Number," from Mr. Fantasy (Island 1968)

White Noise, "An Electric Storm" (Island 1969)

McDonald and Giles, "McDonald and Giles" (Island 1970)

Nick Drake, "The River Man," from *Five Leaves Left* (Island 1969)

Fairport Convention, "Meet on the Ledge," from What We Did on Our Holidays" (Island 1968)

Nirvana, "Tiny Goddess," from *All of Us* (Jimmy Miller mix, Island 1969)

Free, *Tons of Sobs* (Island 1968)

THE RECORDS I LIKED TO LISTEN TO THEN (AND STILL LIKE TO LISTEN TO TODAY)

. . . In No Specific Order

The Appletree Theatre, *Playback* (1967)

Love, *Forever Changes* (1967)

Ravi Shankar, *Portrait of a Genius* (1964)

Jimmy Reed, *Jimmy Reed at Carnegie Hall (1968); Just Jimmy Reed (1962); Jimmy Reed at Soul City* (1964)

Bob Dylan, *Highway 61 Revisited (1965); Blonde on Blonde* (1966)

Jefferson Airplane, *Surrealistic Pillow* (1966)

Big Brother and the Holding Company, *Big Brother and the Holding Company (1967); Cheap Thrills* (1968)

The Jimi Hendrix Experience, *Are You Experienced (1967); Axis: Bold as Love* (1968); Electric Ladyland (1968)

Captain Beefheart, *Trout Mask Replica* (1969)

Frank Zappa and the Mothers of Invention, *Freak Out (1966); Cruisin' with Ruben and the Jets* (1968)

Mose Allison, *I Love the Life I Live (1960); Mose Allison Sings (1963); Swingin' Machine* (1963)

Chuck Berry, *After School Session* (1957)

The Incredible String Band, *The 5000 Spirits on the*

Layer of the Onion (1967)

Otis Redding, *Pain in my Heart* (early-1960s compilation)

The Move, *The Move* (1968)

The Zombies, *Odyssey and Oracle* (1968)

The Beatles, *Revolver* (1966)

The Misunderstood, *Before the Dream Faded* (1966)

The Byrds, *The Notorious Byrd Brothers (1968);* Sweetheart of the Rodeo (1968)

The Beach Boys, *Wild Honey* (1967)

The Flying Burrito Brothers, *The Gilded Palace of Sin* (1969)

Paul Butterfield Blues Band, *Paul Butterfield Blues Band* (1965)

Cream, *Disraeli Gears* (1967)

Count Five, *Psychotic Reaction* (1966)

Sagittarius, *Present Tense* (1968)

Ray Charles, *A Man and His Soul* (1967)

Memphis Slim and Willie Dixon, *In Paris* (1962)

Hair, cast album from the musical (1968)

The Reverend Gary Davis, *Samson and Delilah* (1956)

The Animals, *Animalism* (1966)

Charles Mingus, *Oh Yeah* (1962)

NOTHING CHANGES OR DOES IT?

The sky, the town and the river

The statues, the fears and the dreams

The leaving, the search and the longing

The questions, the lies and the tears

Nothing changes or does it?

The dance hall, the school and the sports field

The stories, the laughter, the drink

The passion, the books and the music

The family, the priests and the wink

Nothing changes or does it?

The church, the factory, the pool hall

The arch, the fog and the mist

The stars, the stage and the players

The knife, the boot and the fist

Nothing changes or does it?

The truth, the guilt and the sorrow

The space, the flowers and the rain

The soul, the heart and the silence

The blues, the money, the pain

Nothing changes or does it?

The pills, the smoke and the fucking,

The trips, the road and the tribes

The love, the smiles and the children

The women, the friends and the wives

Nothing changes or does it?

The sacred, the psychic, the demon

The mystery, the thoughts and the need

The words, the tunes and the language

The obsessions, the questions, the deeds

Nothing changes or does it?

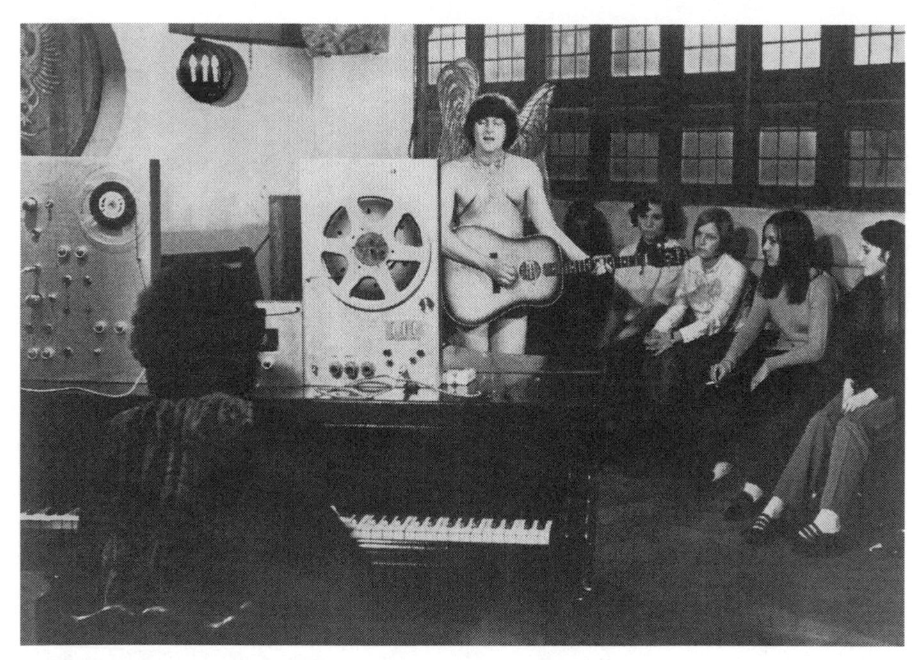

What's next for Patrick Campbell-lyons?

The 13 Dalis, an exciting new CD coming in 2010. Stay tuned to www.psychedelicdays.com for details.

Made in the USA
Charleston, SC
17 February 2011